"Rick Bragg spins his mesmerizing tales of life down South with characteristically wry humor and wisdom. . . . *The Speckled Beauty* takes its place beside Willie Morris's *My Dog Skip*, Marjorie Kinnan Rawlings's animal narratives and William Faulkner's dog stories . . . confirming once more Bragg's enduring artfulness and cracking good ability to spin memorable, affectionate tales."

—*BookPage* (starred review)

"Amid dark days, bright Speck shows up at just the right time. How fortunate for readers that the joy of his presence—enhanced by the wit and wisdom of Bragg's inimitable prose—will resonate far beyond the Bragg homestead."   —*Shelf Awareness*

"Bragg's story will resonate with dog lovers and with his many fans, who will recognize this book's enjoyably colloquial tone from his monthly essays in *Southern Living* magazine."

— *Library Journal* (starred review)

Rick Bragg

THE SPECKLED BEAUTY

Rick Bragg is the author of twelve books, including the bestselling *Ava's Man* and *All Over but the Shoutin'*. He is also a regular contributor to *Garden & Gun* magazine and *Southern Living*. He lives in Alabama.

Rick Bragg is available for select speaking engagements. To inquire about a possible speaking appearance, please contact Penguin Random House Speakers Bureau at speakers@penguinrandomhouse.com or visit prhspeakers.com.

THE SPECKLED BEAUTY

THE SPECKLED BEAUTY

A Dog and His People

Rick Bragg

THE SPECKLED BEAUTY

A Dog and His People

Rick Bragg

VINTAGE BOOKS

A DIVISION OF PENGUIN RANDOM HOUSE LLC

NEW YORK

FIRST VINTAGE BOOKS EDITION 2022

Copyright © 2021 by Rick Bragg

All rights reserved. Published in the United States
by Vintage Books, a division of Penguin Random House LLC,
New York, and distributed in Canada by Penguin Random House
Canada Limited, Toronto. Originally published in hardcover in the
United States by Alfred A. Knopf, a division of Penguin
Random House LLC, New York, in 2021.

Vintage and colophon are registered
trademarks of Penguin Random House LLC.

The Library of Congress has cataloged the Knopf edition as follows:
Names: Bragg, Rick, author.
Title: The speckled beauty : a dog and his people / Rick Bragg.
Description: First edition. | New York : Alfred A. Knopf, 2021.
Identifiers: LCCN 2020043810 (print) | LCCN 2020043811 (ebook)
Subjects: LCSH: Bragg, Rick. | Dog owners—Biography. | Pet loss.
Classification: LCC SF422.82.B73 A3 2021 (print) |
LCC SF422.82.B73 (ebook) | DDC 636.70092 B—dc23
LC record available at https://lccn.loc.gov/2020043810
LC ebook record available at https://lccn.loc.gov/2020043811

Vintage Books Trade Paperback ISBN: 978-0-593-08141-9
eBook ISBN: 978-0-525-65882-5

Book design by Maggie Hinders

vintagebooks.com

Printed in the United States of America
1st Printing

For Sam

Who wants a perfect dog?

—WILLIE MORRIS

Contents

INTRODUCTION
Guilty as Sin and One Eye Shining   3

ONE   *The Dog I Had in Mind*   25

TWO   *Squirrels Beyond Measure*   39

THREE   *Tough Guys*   51

FOUR   *Pandemonium*   62

FIVE   *Geraldine*   74

SIX   *Jackasses*   83

SEVEN   *Big Deal*   94

EIGHT   *In a Lake of Fire*   109

NINE   *Tumbling, Tumbling Down*   122

TEN   *Magic Dogs*   135

ELEVEN   *When Dogs Will Fly*   153

CONTENTS

TWELVE *Dog Days* 163

THIRTEEN *The Return of Henry* 180

FOURTEEN *Of Mules and Men* 190

FIFTEEN *Quarantine* 215

SIXTEEN *Boomers* 224

EPILOGUE *Light Sleeper* 229

Acknowledgments 241

THE SPECKLED BEAUTY

Guilty as Sin and One Eye Shining

THE DRIVEWAY is a winding quarter mile, a dim, green tunnel through tangled pines and mountain pasture, fractured by dappled sunlight on the clear, hot days. Flashes of color, of blue jays, yellowhammers, and an emerald blur of hummingbirds, crisscross the rusted barbed wire, and mockingbirds touch down on cedar posts that were cut from this mountain one hundred years before. Whitetail deer and wild turkeys, like periscopes, spy over tall, sharp blades of Johnsongrass, and white egrets, rare here in the red dirt, up so high, pose on one leg in the flat, brown water of the pond. And it all seems painted on, somehow, as if someone dreamed it up on a slow day with an easy mind and hung it on the air. Then *he* rumbles in, and goes to raising all kinds of hell.

The dog, running half blind, tongue out, and wide open, intercepts my truck halfway up the drive, as the wild things scatter to the corners of the earth. He yowls, twists, and bounces to a hard stop right on some mark only he can find, usually smack-dab in a red-ant bed or mudhole but always safely away from the main road, as if he can remember all the meanness and suffering there and knows this mountain is his sanctuary, and his last stand. *Run too far, and you fall off the world.* I know this is reading a lot into a dog who falls asleep in his food bowl, suffers a shivering apoplexy when you rub his belly, and acts as if every wayward possum is a sign of the end of times. But I don't think any dog knows home better than one thrown away once already.

This is, though, pretty much the sum of his comprehension. He seems to forget every waking day that a one-ton truck is not to be messed with, and, biting at the spinning tires, tries to herd it up the drive like a big, sparkly cow. "He'll move," people say, because everyone is an expert when it's not their dog in the road. But I can never recall which side his bad eye is on, so I stomp the brake and twist the wheel and finally, lurching, cursing, arrive at the cabin at the top of the hill. I swing open the door, and the dog, seventy-six pounds of

wet hair and poor decisions, lunges in, eternally
surprised, and overjoyed, that it is me. I yell "Get
DOWN!" but too late. The truck's cab is tattooed
in dirt, mud, or biting ants, because he needs to
squirm to within an inch of my face to be sure. I
might have been UPS, or the man from Cherokee
Electric, who has learned to bring a stick.

Then, with a growl, he is off to molest the
livestock, and stir a general panic. He is a herding
dog by blood, an illegitimate Australian shepherd,
and he bolts into the pasture to create a small
stampede. He evades the thumping hooves by
inches, but always gets caught up in a never-
ending circle and cannot find his way out, like a
drunk teenager doing doughnuts in a parking lot.
I stumble after him, yelling, threatening, and he
hunkers down and covers his eyes with his paws.
I used to think he did it out of shame, but now I
think he believes this makes him invisible.

Recently, I came home from a week-long trip
to find the driveway peaceful and empty, the
terrible dog nowhere around. It always made me
a little nervous when he didn't rush down to meet
me; as much as any creature I have ever known,
he has lived a blink away from destruction. My
brother Sam was in the barn beating on an old
Yanmar tractor with a hammer. It had run hot

again and scalded him, so he was ill tempered and short, which is his most natural state. I don't know if he was working on it, or just getting even.

"You seen my dog?" I asked.

"He's in jail . . . ," he said.

BAM!

". . . again."

In the dog's first month here, he was incarcerated twenty-nine times. Telling him to behave, even after almost two years now, is like telling him it is Tuesday.

"What," I asked, "did he do now?"

"Run the mule," he said.

I told him that was not so bad, a dog running one solitary mule.

"Run the mule. Run the donkeys. Run 'em half to death. Run 'em round 'n' round the pasture, bitin' at their legs . . . run 'em till they went to blowin' 'n' buckin' 'n' screamin' 'n' tried to kick him to death. Don't know where he wanted 'em to go. Don't think he did."

BAM!

"What else?" I asked, because there was always something else.

"Dragged part of an old, dead deer up to the house . . . stunk worse than anything I ever smelt . . . Laid there chewing on a leg bone by the kitchen window . . . You can still smell it."

He paused to let his contempt gather, like an old, creaky train cresting a hill.

"Picked a fight with Momma's puppy. Stole the puppy's ball 'n' took it off and buried it . . . When I fed 'em he wouldn't let the puppy eat. Went 'n' laid in the puppy's bowl, 'n' growled."

BAM!

BAM!

BAM!

He pointed to a puddle in the middle of the garage floor. "Peed on the tractor. Peed on my truck. Peed on Momma's flowers . . ." The zinnias looked like they had been poisoned.

". . . so Momma told me to lock him up."

He set down the hammer and picked up a wrench. He twisted it, grimly, on a rusted bolt, like he was tightening a noose, and realized he had left something out.

"Eat all the cat food Momma put out . . . cats flyin' ever'where."

I laughed and he shot me a dirty look. He does not even like the cats, which are too well fed to catch mice and have no practical use; how he must loathe my dog, to take the side of a cat.

He went back to abusing the tractor, mumbling

around a big dip of snuff. I could only make out about every third word, but the gist, I believe, was that I never should have let the dog take root here in the first place, should have run him off immediately and permanently with a handful of rocks. A pitiful stray is one thing; you can save a gentle stray. But a dog like this, wild for so long, would bring only woe. He didn't say "woe," but that was what he meant. Sometimes, when my dog walked too close to him, he spit on his head.

Sam owned only obedient, serious dogs, and there is no room in his mind for a dog that cannot work for a living, or do what it is told. He grew up in a time when even the best dogs lived at the end of a logging chain and ate from an upside-down hubcap; he dosed their mange with burnt motor oil, and dressed their wounds in kerosene. They were throwaway dogs, too, earless, toothless, chewed on, stitched up, and gun-shy, but they loaded themselves into the truck's dog box without being told, trailed a scent across miles and mountains, and stayed on a tree till he kicked them off it. His dogs would swim a river for him; all he had to do was whistle.

"You got to train a dog, got to make 'em mind," he said, making it plain that everything wrong with my dog was my fault. I had tried to train the dog, for months, for years, but had miserably failed. Giving him a command of any kind was fruitless, bordering on stupid. I might as well read him *The Song of Hiawatha*, or sing "On Wisconsin." I had to heave him into the truck like a sack of fertilizer every time I took him to the veterinarian, that or lure him in with cold cuts.

Fancy dog people, the ones who play fetch with their pets in German and feed them only healthy, joyless food, said I should speak to him in a deep, strong voice, to show him I was the alpha male. If this failed, they said, I should smack him smartly on the nose with a rolled-up newspaper. But they have not met my dog. He has the attention span of a tick on a hot rock, and by the time I found a newspaper and rolled it up, he would not remember what he was being punished for. I would just be a big, mean man beating a befuddled dog with a Walmart circular.

"You could beat him with a stick of firewood," my brother said, but he was kidding, I am almost sure.

"Or," he said, "a short length of two-by-four."

The pen was, I guess, more humane.

"How did y'all lure him in?" I asked.

My mother's disembodied voice came from the other side of the screen door.

"I made him a mayonnaise sandwich," she said, "and he walked right in."

"I guess there was nothing else to do, then," I said.

"He wet on my sweet Williams," my mother's voice said.

"I know," I said. "I'm sorry."

There was no answer; she had moved on. The dog even had me apologizing to a screen door.

It was the grave robbing, my brother said, that sealed it. They could forgive the rest of it, even a certain amount of careless urination; he was a boy dog, after all. But if there was a corpse of any kind close by, one left lying by a careless deer hunter or hastily covered over by some poacher, he would find it, dig it up, drag it here, and gnaw on it, till I took it away, gagging. The closest human cemetery was, blessedly, several miles away, so it was always a four-legged cadaver of some kind that he brought us. Still, I sometimes wondered if I would come home one evening to find him tugging, by the dress hem, someone's dear, departed Aunt Lurleen.

Anyway, I'd had about all the lecture I could stand. Once, when we were boys, he would have understood why I wanted this dog, but I guess the grouchy old man couldn't see it anymore.

"I will say one thing for him," said my brother,

a good man despite that stiff back and hard head. "He ain't got no fear in him . . ." The dog would not back down from a rattlesnake.

He whacked the old tractor one last, good lick, so it would know better next time.

". . . n'r brains, neither."

I got a flashlight from my truck and followed the circle of light down the path to the pen. When you walked here, in hot weather, you walked in a kind of Southern rain forest, amidst the creeping vines and poison ivy and the big black-and-yellow spiders, webs dripping silver in air so heavy it seemed to be held up by faith alone. The hum of insects and trilling of frogs, a million at least, sang out of the dark, and glowing specks of lightning bugs winked on and off. They were flying low that night, just above the high grass; my grandma used to say that meant it was going to rain. And there in that twinkling light, guilty as sin and one eye shining, was my dog.

His left eye, a light brown, reflected the light in the way a dog's eyes are supposed to do. But his right eye was an almost solid blue-black, and the light from the flashlight beam just seemed to soak into it, to disappear, as if you were shining it down a well. He was mostly blind in that eye, and sometimes, if he turned too fast to that side, he ran headfirst into a fence post, or a tree, or the side of a moving pickup truck. A thin, black scar, no thicker than the line from a felt-tip pen, ran just above and below the eye, like a claw mark. And I wondered if that wound was the reason someone threw him away, or if it happened later, when he was fighting for his life in the hobo jungle.

But the mismatched eyes did not ruin his face; they just made him look like the pirate he is. He has the striking mottled coat specific to his bloodline, a mix of blue, red, gray, black, brown, and white, with copper points, like freckles, dotting his white face and paws. My mother called it his Coat of Many Colors, from the Bible, but I told her I was pretty sure that scripture had nothing to do with it. Still, he could look almost noble, from a distance, till you got close enough to see what the world had done to him, and to discern that he had recently rolled in something terrible.

He sat at the gate, unmoving, silent, watching the trail. He can see all right in daylight on his good side, but the dusk is hard. He cannot catch a bouncing ball or follow a bird on the wing; his depth perception is too poor for that, and it is even harder for him in the half-light. His hearing is also sketchy; both ears were torn at the skull in his last serious dogfight, though, by some miracle, he can always hear the words "snack" and "biscuit." Even his sense of smell is a little blunted; he will walk right over a fried chicken liver if he loses sight of it in flight, but he can eat twenty of them, easy, with a side of fries and some yeast rolls, from a paper plate on the porch.

He heard me coming in the dark and barked, but just once, his voice hoarse and tortured. He had been wounded there, too, his neck and throat hurt in some old battle, and he had tender places in his ribs, one hip, and spine, where we think he was hit by at least one car. But he was no invalid, no broke-down dog; he was strong, fast, always hungry, always scrounging. Today, he had been hollered at, kicked at, and cussed sideways, and that was just since midafternoon, but he did not sulk or whine. He knew I was coming; I broke him out every night, about this time.

"I see you, buddy," I said from the dark.

"I see you."

He leapt as high as he could, once, twice, three times, then hurled himself at the chain link and tried to turn some kind of pitiful, ragged flip. But he never got much more than sideways, so I guess it was more a spin. Then he crouched, his feet beating a tattoo in the dirt, his tail going like an eggbeater. I reached through a gap in the gate and pulled on his mismatched ears.

"Who's a good buddy?" I said, and he told me, with every thump of his tail, every quiver, that *he* was. I had my hand on the latch when I heard the accusing screech of the screen door.

"Do *not* let him out," my mother called from the porch. She is eighty-three years old and has rescued dozens of unwanted and damaged dogs, but she has never suffered a fool such as this.

"I won't," I promised, and the door banged shut like a gavel coming down. The dog looked at me, just happy to be alive. Who can bear to see that in a cage?

He took off like a shotgun blast, throwing up whorls of dead leaves and dust. He tore around the cabin, then again, and again, till you could hear him breathing hard on every lap. Cats, again, exploded from every crevice, and every faraway dog for three miles began to yap and howl. I thought he might actually run himself to death, before he finally came to some sense. On his fourth lap, he staggered up and leaned against my leg. I sat in an old lawn chair and rubbed his head; it was Jacksonville, Alabama, on a weekday night, and I sure as hell didn't have anything better to do. Then I heard the screech of the door, again.

"Hide," I told him, and he tore off again through the trees.

"You let him out, didn't you?" my mother and brother asked, almost in stereo, when I came in the kitchen. I started to lie, but the evidence was looking at us through the screen door.

"I told you to hide," I told him.

He rolled over and presented his belly, in case anyone wanted to rub it. His tongue hung out the side of his head. It was the only trick he was any good at; "sit" and "stay" were, as yet, impossible dreams.

"Put your tongue back in your head," my mother ordered.

Nothing.

"Nobody wants to see that," she said.

Nothing.

He rolled to his feet, or tried. The edge of the porch was on his blind side and he stumbled to the steps with all the grace of a rocking horse banging down a flight of stairs. He leapt into the air like he was on springs, as if to show us it was all just part of the act. It made me think of when I was a boy, running around in a cape cut from a dish towel, shouting "Ta-da!" after I tripped on my own untied shoelaces and face-planted into the floor.

I told him he was a good boy, ignoring the

rolling of eyes inside the house, and closed the door. He waited at the steps for a minute or two, in case it should reopen and someone would start handing out some reward. It is my fault he lives in this delusion. He believes he *is* a good boy, because of the thousands of times I have lied and told him so. He may not understand much else, may not even know which way "up" is, but he almost levitates when he hears those words; then, he could be thinking about squirrels, or scrambled eggs.

After a while he turned and trotted off into the trees. He usually slept in the same place, in a thick copse of hardwoods at the pasture gate, in case the jackasses, which he never trusted to begin with, should stage an escape, or a revolt, as jackasses are known to do.

I had tried to gentrify the dog. I tried to get him to sleep in the garage or on the porch, but he refused; he was not a dog that compromised. I gave him blankets, but he dragged them through saw briers and effluviums, and they were never, not one thread, seen again. I bought him a $150 dog bed, and he lost his mind, snatched it from my hands before I could get it out of the box, and went into a weird African death roll, with me clinging to the other end. We played a grim tug-of-war with the empty cover, for pride, I guess, as the stuffing wafted down like snow. The dog calmed down only when I draped it over his head, like a crazed horse in a burning barn.

That night, like most nights, he woke me four or five times, barking insanely at creatures, real and imagined, out in the trees. The last time, about 3:00 a.m., I gave up and went outside to sit on the porch steps, calling to him to please hush, for God's sake, which only made him bawl and yowl even louder. He came leaping out of the dark to almost knock me down, to let me know he was still on the job, and that, next time, it could be a bear.

I didn't sleep, anyway. I had been ill, with the blood cancer non-Hodgkin's lymphoma. Everyone said it was the best kind to get, like I was buying a washing machine, and after years of treatment, sitting beside brave people who had lost everything, I was in remission. I had good doctors, and people praying who, unlike me, would not burst into flame. But the chemo made me stupid, and a litany of miseries—heart and kidney failure, pneumonia, more—beat me down. I drove myself to an ER one night, smothering. I lived in waiting rooms, counting needles, reading two-year-old *Field & Streams*. I piled up kidney stones like they were money, and jabbed myself with a needle of insulin twice a day to pay for an ice-cream cone I had in '73. On top of that, old nerve damage in one ear left me with a keening that was murder late at night. Doctors said I was depressed, and I thought, *Well, hell, I reckon so.* But those meds made me stupid, too, so I quit. I needed to feel something when I struck a key. I never asked, though, *Why me?* I'd made a living writing of other people's sadness, in harder times than this. It was my turn.

I got better, but not all the way back. I couldn't remember the last good decision I made or promise I kept. The truth is that I had come to think of my life as a story I had already finished, and everything left was just a dull waiting, like cocktail hour at a Howard Johnson's. I guess it happens to a lot of people.

The celebrated Texas writer Larry McMurtry made it sound almost like poetry. He wrote of a young frontiersman who lived a rich, sweeping life, but always felt an emptiness in him, winding through. Some men were just born beside a river of melancholy. Some men lived a lifetime there. It sounded romantic when I was a young man, till the day I woke up and it was as real as rocks, or rain. You never know what you will find to care about, by a river like that.

The dog sat on the steps beside me; he smelled faintly of carrion.

"Good boy."

•

He is still an outside dog, mostly, but he will come in during a thunderstorm, or if he hears the faraway boom of a shotgun, or when he just gets lonesome. He stays inside for just half an hour or so, usually, before he begins to pace and fret. He runs to the door, rears up to place his paws on the glass, and stares out at the big adventure on the other side. Think what he might miss while he is curled on the couch, or rug, waiting for his stupid human to set him free; think of all the things, dark and dangerous, left to roam his mountain, unseen. If I am too slow, he cranks his head around to glare at me, frantic, disappointed. *Don't you know? Don't you know what's out there? BOOGERS! Boogers by the THOUSANDS!* The inside of the kitchen door is covered with deep grooves and scratches, from his impatience. It was such a nice door, before.

He is inside as I write this, under my feet, because that is the most inconvenient place for him to be. He is destroying a towel he dragged off the bathroom wall, pinning it to the floor with his paws and ripping it to doll rags. I tried to give him an old, threadbare towel to play with, but he ignored it, trotted into the bathroom, and tugged another one off the wall. It is the stealing, then, that makes it better; there is just no flavor in a towel unstole. After a while, I started placing the same unspeakable towel on the wall, so he will think he is stealing it over and over again. Sometimes it works, and sometimes it doesn't; I am locked in a battle of wits with a creature who thinks his twin brother lives inside a shiny hubcap, and pitches a fit over the color red.

He will rise occasionally, stretch, yawn, and go drink noisily and imprecisely from the toilet. I know I could simply close the door, but it is such a heartwarming thing, a dog with his nose in the toilet, penned there by the seat that has dropped down around his ears. He growls and pulls, oblivious to the fact that this is all his fault; he believes he has been assaulted by the dreaded potty monster, again. But how do you not love a dog with a toilet-seat halo around his head?

I watch him snarl and thrash, and think of the old men I used to follow around when I was a boy, the backslid Bible scholars, day-drinkers, and Huddle House philosophers who chain-smoked

Lucky Strikes and educated me on black racers, bad whiskey, and why the Baptists were going to hell in a handcar. And, on every other breath, they told me stories about dogs. The old talkers are mostly gone now, laid to rest under a few inadequate words gouged into a granite slab; no one should have to tell a story with a chisel, which does not allow for exaggeration, adjustment, or lies. But, my God, the stories they could have told about my boy.

So, I guess it's on me. To be truthful, I always wanted to write about a dog with a story to tell. I think a lot of writers do, the ones who have a soul; the rest are cat people, I suppose.

I worried, at first, that my buddy would be unfit company for those heroic dogs that live in literature, in books like Jack London's *Call of the Wild* and *White Fang,* and Fred Gipson's *Old Yeller* and *Savage Sam.* Those dogs dragged sleds across pack ice, battled bears and javelina hogs and marauding renegades, and helped feed their hungry humans even if they had to starve themselves; my dog would battle me to the death over the last cold tater tot.

He is not even a good bad dog. Bad dogs in literature were lovable rogues, not recidivists like mine; you could put a hat on them, or reindeer antlers, and ride them around in a Subaru. Little children could ride on them, like a pony, and teach them to do the *cha-cha-cha*. They loved babies, and licked them into giggling fits; if I saw my dog take a taste of an unattended baby, my heart would die in my chest.

I know I couldn't get someone to steal him if I stuck a thousand dollars to him with hairpins, yet I would not sell him at any price. You can't buy a dog like this, anyway. If you want one, you have to wait for this sorry ol' world to make it, as it did mine. He will not play fetch or shake hands, submit to a bath or take his medicine, even if it is concealed in a sausage biscuit. But he will dig a snake out of a gopher hole or chase a landfill rat across a smoking ruin, to live another day. If you want one, you have to adopt the sorriest mutt in the pound, or get one out of the trash.

He was probably just a dog, once, but that was only the humdrum beginning of things. He was abandoned at the side of the road, because he was damaged, or inconvenient. He ran with the strays, lived in ditches and dumps and pulpwood barrens for a year or more, a king of the damned, till they turned on him, tore him up, and drove him out. He wandered, getting hungrier, weaker, searching for a life that must have faded a little more with every passing day. I am not saying there is magic in it, only that he soaked up all that hurt to come here, to stampede the jackasses and do somersaults in a cage. He is so reckless that I hold my breath, waiting for his borrowed time to run out, and he rushes on, leading with his good eye, boring through blackberry bushes, saw briars, and barbed wire. I don't know; maybe he thinks he finally made it back, after all.

Maybe we will even call it a saga, since a saga, in dog years, does not have to be much of a saga at all.

I still wish, sometimes, for a good dog. A good dog would be a fine thing to have on a regular day. But I believe it takes a bad dog to gnaw, scratch, and rip at an empty one. It takes a dog that has survived low-down, dirty meanness to make a river of melancholy seem like one more mudhole to splash through. He can turn that bad eye on you, that eye that has no bottom to its suffering, and make you ashamed of such a puny human frailty as that. Oh, I still feel it, like a lot of people, rushing, pushing by, and maybe I always will. But I believe he is doing all he can, and it's best not to ask too much of a creature still captive in the commode.

It took awhile but we finally gave him a name. We call him Speck, for short, though I am still not sure if he knows this is his name to keep, or if his old one, the one we will never know, still bounces around inside his skull. But he stays out of the road, and my brother has promised to stop spitting on his head.

ONE

The Dog I Had in Mind

2019

THE CAT in the waiting room looked us over, suspicious and superior. That's the way a cat will do you.

I sat with my dog, and worried. That morning, he had a bad, shaking cough, and choked when he tried to breathe. I heaved him, kicking, protesting, into the back seat of my pickup, and rushed him to the vet.

I thought he had just swallowed something unspeakable, and with this dog that could have been anything from a live toad to a welding glove. That, or he was just sick, or poisoned; there was no telling what terrible disease he might have picked up, toting a jawbone around for a chew toy.

He had been my dog for about two years now, and had ingested things I cannot even say.

He was stuck fast to my knee, again. This did not mean I was his master, merely his alibi, coconspirator, bailsman, and the driver of his ambulance. Most people would have taken comfort in the fact their dog stuck so close to them. These people, I suspect, are not familiar with the term "guilt by association."

The nurse called his name, and I dragged him to the exam room on a leash. On the way he tried to water the dog food display like it was my mother's calla lilies, but I snatched him back. He gave the cat a look as we passed by.

Don't be here when I get back, Fluffy.

I don't like to read too much into the dog, and I don't like to pretend to speak for him, but in the two years or so since he arrived some things are just easy to translate.

In the exam room, he coughed so hard he seemed to vibrate, but wagged his tail, unconcerned. He is *not* a good boy, but he is a tough boy, and this was just one more scrap for him, just one more fight in a ditch.

The vet, Dr. Eric Clanton, called his cough "violent," and decided to do an X-ray to see if something was stuck in his windpipe. The nurse

gave him a shot to knock him out, because it
was not in his nature to behave or hold still just
because someone asked him to, and he lay on the
floor as the drug took effect, goofy and kind of lost.

"That's the best he's behaved since I got him," I
told the nurses, trying to sound tough, but it broke
my heart to see him like that. I reached down
and rubbed his head, but he was out cold now,
snuffling and drooling on the floor.

He is not the dog I had in mind.

I had in mind a good dog, in all the usual ways.

•

Just a few weeks before, I had been half asleep
in a deep chair with a novel, *The Italian Secretary*
by Caleb Carr, open on my chest. The television
was on, the sound turned low. Rita Hayworth was
singing a torch song and dancing in her bare feet. I
could hear the dog outside, his bark fading in and
out, drowning in the hollers, rising on the ridge.
I remember there was a big, orange moon that
night, almost like daylight. The dog went wackier
than usual under a moon like that.

My sixtieth birthday had passed without a
parade, but I was feeling old, used up, and
no-account long before I approached that

milestone. I had been falling apart and glued back together for some time, tired, grouchy, and confused, and still five years shy of what people here call their old-age pension. My excellent doctors, all eleven or twelve, told me I was damaged, undisciplined, self-destructive, probably doomed, and maybe maladjusted, but in no immediate peril. I might limp on a ways, with clean living and fine insurance. But this was not a walk I wanted to take on my own. I thought it might be nice, on this leg of the journey, to have an old, slow, easy dog to go with me.

I had in mind a fat dog, a gentle plodder that only slobbered an acceptable amount and would not chase a car even if the trunk was packed with pork chops. In my mind, we shuffled side by side along a smooth path that was always slightly downhill, in a season that was always sweatshirt weather, always just right. In the chest pocket of my old, frayed button-down there was always a fresh pack of Juicy Fruit; you will go through more than you would think, going no place special. In my mind, I had traded my boots and jeans for some spongy orthopedic shoes and a baggy pair of corduroy trousers; I always planned on getting some when I was too old to care. Here, in this easy make-believe, I always had an apple in my pocket, and a full bag of treats. A good dog, especially a fat one, will need a treat every mile or so. And together, my old dog and I would shuffle off into the sunset, though we might have to stop occasionally, for a nap.

I have always loved that notion that dogs bring out the best in us, and have always wanted to believe in something like that. Sometimes, when the melancholy is on me, I get a little lost in the bitter weeds, and I see a much more likely end for a man like me. I see one of those mean old men who rock angry on an unpainted porch, glaring off into the great might-have-been. I can almost hear the runners squeal, hear the old man screech at the passersby that, as soon as he can get straightened up good, he will come down off that porch and kick their asses up to their watch pockets.

But I can't picture it, somehow, with an old, slow, easy dog close by. It would make me ashamed of myself, in a way that most people never had.

Maybe we would even shuffle off down to some clear lake and pretend to fish, beside a bottomless cooler of bologna sandwiches and ice-cold root beer; maybe that is what heaven is. We might not even bait a hook, might just kick back and enjoy the day. If, by some miracle, we should catch a fish,

we will just ease it back into the water. And if we
see a snake, we will let it be.

It always seemed like a reasonable thing, not
a dream but a modest plan. I know it might not
sound like much to someone who wants to dive
with the sharks on their one hundredth birthday,
or hike a volcano on a new hip. I'm just telling you
the dog I had in mind, for the shape I was in.

Outside, I could still hear my crazy dog chasing
the wind through the trees.

Midnight passed, then one, two . . . I think I had
just closed my eyes.

Yalp! Yalp! Yalp! Grrrrrrrrrrrrr . . .

Speck.

His tone was different this time, urgent, angry.
My older brother, who has a fine way with words,
calls it a booger bark; you heard it in a dog's voice
when he was truly spooked, not just interested
in some wayward coon or wandering deer. Some
dogs, you can ignore in times like this; you can
leave them to their silliness till the threat moves
away, or the dog just runs down, like a child's
battery-powered toy. Some dogs, you can. I have
seen Speck run himself into staggering exhaustion,
over a possibility. *It better be a rhinoceros,* I thought
as I pulled on my shoes.

I was surprised to see him at the foot of the hill,

bouncing in place, waiting for me to catch up. That worried me a little; he never waited for me to catch up. As soon as he saw me in the porch light he took off again, running not into the trees that formed a horseshoe around the cabin, which was where he usually played in the dark, but straight down the driveway and toward the road, as fast as he could go. I followed him around a sharp dogleg that hid the cabin from the road. And there in the driveway, a few yards from the mailbox, I saw the red glow of a single taillight.

The car, an old import, had backed into the drive, its engine idling. I eased up behind it, thinking what a sad end it would be to get shot dead in my fuzzy house shoes in my own driveway. I should have had a flashlight, but I didn't think I needed one just to step outside and cuss out a barking dog. I stopped, not sure what to do next. Of all the hateful things that descended on me in the years after getting sick, a wretched and feeble uncertainty was the worst.

Once, it all would have seemed harmless to me. Teenagers pulled into the dark drive to park, sometimes, but it appeared that this was not young love taking its course, or kids passing a joint. Meth had left a stain on life down here, and no one said, anymore, that they didn't lock their doors.

I saw the spike of a lighter, and then again, and again . . . The old car seemed to sag with people. I imagined skinned heads and neck tattoos, but they could have been Amway salesmen or Jehovah's Witnesses for all I knew, or nuns. But they shouldn't have messed with my dog.

He was bouncing at the driver's side door, growling, furious, and I could hear the people inside laugh at him through the cracked windows of the car. Speck yowled at the glass, close enough to fog it with his breath. I heard an anemic electric window groan down and saw something fly out of it, then heard a yelp and the unmistakable *thunk* and *tinkle* of a beer bottle, not shattering but rolling in the grass and gravel. They were throwing bottles at my dog.

A dog with any sense would have run away, but I guess all they did was make him mad. I called him, once, twice, almost in a whisper.

Nothing.

I picked up the first dead limb I saw in the gloom. I was not particular.

I stepped up closer to the car, almost to the back bumper, and called again, in that inane way that people try to whisper as loud as they can.

"Speck! Here!" I hissed.

Nothing.

I took one or two steps more, to within a few feet of the car's rear window. What I meant to say, what I had in my mind to say, was a stern, reasonable:

Y'all need to ease on out of here, right now.

What came out, instead, was a shrill, angry:

"I'll kill y'all, if y'all hurt my dog."

I didn't recognize my own voice; I think, maybe, I used to know the redneck who said crazy stuff like that, who believed he *could* say things like that, then absorb the consequences, but that leaping dumbass was surely dead and gone by now. But you see, I didn't have any choice. Even if he is the worst dog of all time, he is *my* dog; you don't throw beer bottles at a man's dog, and giggle. You can't try to hurt a man's dog right in front of him and get away with it.

I remember thinking, as I stood there, that I wished I had selected a bigger and better twig, but there are just some stupidities that, once committed to, just have to be seen through.

I waited for the doors to swing open and the ass whipping—mine, most likely—to commence, but I guess no one in that car of late-night party people was as stupid as I was. I saw the weeds glow red behind the car as the driver toed the brake and slammed the transmission into drive. Speck danced out of the way just as the car belched a whorl of smoke and lurched away, tires and fan belt screeching. The old car made a hard right on the main road and disappeared.

"Yeah, y'all better run," I yelled, bravely, once I was sure they were, indeed, running. The dog, overjoyed, sang a song of belligerence in a cloud of wafting smut.

I guess they thought I had a pistol; this is Alabama, where pretty much everyone does. People go armed to the dentist, choir practice, the PTA, and Ruby Tuesday's; why *not* go armed in your driveway. I did not, in fact, have a pistol, or even real shoes or long pants. But I would have done grievous harm to that windshield until I came to my senses, or got shot, or beaten up, or—and I am not discounting this—got chased back up my own driveway screeching *Call 911!*

I should have known that a dog like mine would lead me into situations like this, as surely as a good dog will lead you away from them. He wanted to chase the trail of smoke, but I hollered at him with all the meanness I could muster; he pulled up after a few steps, not because he was minding me but because of that thing in his head, that compass, that held him to this place.

I got a death grip on his collar and began

dragging him, resisting, back up the drive. I was a little concerned that the people in the car might drink or smoke up some courage and come back here with a gun, and I did not want the dog, or me, to get a second chance at killing ourselves. It was uphill all the way, and he fought me every step. I dragged him up the drive, across the yard, up the steps, and into the house, and along the way I lost a shoe and could not get it back. I was wheezing, croaking, by the time I made it to the door. The dog still wanted to fight somebody, and ran crazily around the cabin, scattering mail and magazines. Ceramic angels trembled on a shelf. My mother, on the edge of her bed, asked if I was all right, asked what was happening, and I just told her, "Dope fiends," since her vernacular of illegal narcotics is frozen in 1952.

"I heard you hollering," she said.

"It was the stupid dog," I said.

I sat in the living room and got my breath, then I got the flashlight and headed for the door.

"What's wrong now?"

"I have to go get my shoe."

The dog walked with me down the drive. He would have torn the door off if I had tried to lock him inside. It was odd, how fast the chaos faded here. I could hear the wind sift in the trees, and the creaking of the limbs. But some of us are not built for tranquility, or the whispering pines.

"I should have busted that damn windshield," I said to the dog.

He looked up, and there it was, that understanding.

Yeah.

"I should have thrown you through the window, and let you at 'em," I told him. "See how long they'd of laughed at you, then, with you in there, *amongst* 'em."

Yeah.

•

The vet was gone only a little while.

He showed me the X-rays. The cartilage that held open the dog's trachea had partially collapsed, causing it to flatten. He could breathe in, but it constricted when he exhaled, trapping his last breath, causing him to sometimes choke and cough.

"Is it fatal," I asked.

The vet shook his head.

"Not necessarily," he said.

The dog was already breathing better, but Dr. Clanton said he was going to keep him overnight, to watch over him, and to run a tube down his throat to make doubly certain there was no blockage there. He was still passed out when I left.

The next day his office called to tell me to come get my dog.

What dog? would have been the prudent response, but I knew they had my address.

He heard my voice and came into the lobby in a rush, almost dancing, the way dogs have done since the beginning of time. He looked fine, and sounded fine, like it never happened. Some dogs, the vet said, just had an amazing ability to reset, to start over the next day. He was that kind of dog.

He gave me some medicine to help with the swelling, but I was hoping for a cure. I wanted him to tell me it would never happen again, that my dog was healed, but I had the wrong dog, entirely, for a guarantee. For now I had my terrible dog back, and I would have to settle for that.

The snooty cat was long gone when we left; the dog looked all around the waiting room for him and seemed bitterly disappointed. To make it up to him, we headed for a fast-food drive-through. I got him a twelve-pack of chicken nuggets and a cup of ice water, and stopped on the town square to feed him. It took twelve seconds, or about one second per nugget. "Can you chew, for God's

sake?" I told him, thinking it would be my luck to
see him survive this most recent catastrophe only
to be choked to death by a Chick-fil-A. People saw
us on the square and stopped by the truck to talk,
or to reach in to pull at his ears or scratch at his
fur. "What a *good boy,*" they said, one after another,
and I just nodded, because who has time to set a
whole town straight?

I had read that dogs like him understand more
than you would think, so I talked as we rolled
toward home. I told him he would get better if he
would take his medicine and not just lick all the
peanut butter off the pill and spit it out on the
kitchen floor. I told him to stop running around
like a crazy dog till he almost passed out, and
to watch himself around the sneaky jackasses,
and the malevolent tomcats, and the dangerous
raccoons, and . . . and then I heard him snore. He
was sound asleep, again, across the back seat. He
huffed, snorted, and growled, in the way dreaming
dogs do. My uncles, who knew a lot about dogs,
used to tell me they were chasing rabbits. But then
I was only a kid, and a kid will believe anything.

TWO

Squirrels Beyond Measure

THE FIRST TIME I saw the dog, he was feasting on a fast-food wrapper in the middle of the road. You don't see many long-haired dogs among the strays, and that alone caught my eye. I was at the mailbox, shuffling bills, junk mail, and a sweepstakes letter telling me congratulations, I was *almost* a billionaire, again. Four or five other strays milled around the long-haired dog, keeping well away from me. They seemed to learn quickly to avoid people, yards, and houses, to realize they lived only on the ragged margins of all that now. I tried not to think about it too much.

There must have been a taste of food left on the paper, because when the others tried to take it he attacked them, snarling, vicious. I scraped up a dirty handful of gravel to throw at them, to run them off or at least chase them out of the blacktop, just as a pickup roared around the curve and, not even slowing down, scattered the strays into the ditches on both sides of the road.

I don't know how it missed them. As it rumbled by, one of the smaller dogs darted into the road, snatched the scrap of paper, and ran for its life, the others strung out behind.

I side-armed the gravel into the road, just glad I didn't see one of them killed. It was January 2017, and I wouldn't have bet a nickel on that long-haired dog to live another month.

It seems my people have always been here, getting saved and shackled and elected and evicted for two hundred years. You get to thinking of a place as yours, after a while, and you grit your teeth over the Red Bull cans and Mountain Dew bottles and takeout chicken bones scattered through one of the prettiest places on earth. But while any half-wit can toss their trash out into a country road, it takes a rarefied, soulless son of a bitch to slink out here to throw away a good dog.

He was still running in the ditches, still fighting over trash and roadkill a few months later. It was the white hair on his freckled face and bushy tail, like a flag, that caught my eye, or I may not have seen him at all. Once these dogs run with the strays awhile, skulking through the ragweed or chasing vermin through the trash, they begin to fade into the litter itself. You see them, but you don't, till you see one crumpled on the asphalt. Then it all gets sharper, meaner, for a while. My brothers noticed him, too, sometimes alone, sometimes with other dogs, miles away.

There was nothing permanent about those packs of strays, just a confederacy of limping mutts, lost beagles, and used-up hounds. They ate everything from eggshells to dirty paper towels, feasted on offal from field-dressed deer, and, if you believed the stories, took the rare pet or newborn calf. I had seen dogs like this all my life, seen them fight to the death over a female in heat, or a few pitiful scraps. It seemed just a matter of time before a stronger, fiercer dog, or the pack, put an end to him, or he just got sick. But I guess he was hard to kill, so we continued to watch for him, my brothers and me. And when we saw him, every few weeks, he was fighting.

The dogs in the pack, if you can call it that, were always disappearing, reappearing, always changing, and sometimes there were no strays at all here that we could see; they left the road and lived in timber tracts or dumps, surviving on rats, snakes, and worse. Most of them were doomed,

sick with tick-borne disease and heartworms,
painted with mange, eaten by fleas.

Sam told me of a coon hunt years ago, when
his dogs led him to a place close to the city dump.
His hunting dogs suddenly bolted and ran hard in
the direction of the truck, ignoring his commands.
"I shined my light around me and there wadn't
nothin' but eyes . . . People would bring cats
they didn't want out to the dump and turn 'em
loose, and the strays would be waitin' to run 'em
down . . . Ain't their fault they get wild like that."
If my brother was uneasy he would not say, it
being him. I guess if they had come too close he
would have swatted them with his hat.

I told him I thought people called them wild,
not strays, because it made them sound dangerous,
made it easier to shoot, trap, even poison them,
and he told me he reckoned so.

But the long-haired dog had a story, a mystery.
He would leave the other dogs and disappear
completely, then rejoin what was left of them
weeks later. Sam believes he was going back, over
and over, to a place in his memory, an abandoned
house or farm, and waiting there for someone
to reappear. Or it might be he was going back to
the place he was left, waiting for his owner to
reappear. "He must've been looking for somebody,"

Sam said. Maybe that is reading a lot into any dog, let alone one like this. None we knew had ever found the person who threw it away. It was a perfect crime; the owner just drove off, taking all the dog had ever known.

Why he always returned so close to the cabin, right here, was a bigger mystery. He was not from here; we would have known if someone was missing this dog. He could have drifted anywhere but always wound up here, like he was trapped inside one more never-ending circle.

We saved a lot of them over the years, mostly the ones that wandered into our yard and were too weak, sick, or hurt to move on. It is how we got Pretty Girl, and Little Girl, and Tick, and Teddy, and Zipper, and at least three Kings. It is how we got Cubby, who was paralyzed on one side, and Reagan, and Floyd, and Little Giz, who was left in a cardboard box. It is how we got Stockings, and Hannibal, and Broken-Hearted Fred, and a hundred others whose names I cannot recall. But we fed and cared for them and they lived easy, with a porch to lie on.

And it is how we got, just in the past few years, the latest refugees, an intelligent and fearless watchdog named Skinny, and a dysfunctional, wild-eyed orphan named Puppy, who seemed to forget he was rescued and had to be won over again every new day. Like all our dogs, they were a kind of antidote for us, for the ones out there we did not save. But Pup and Skinny belonged to my mom, or to the place, not me; they were here when I came home. They made it better, the way dogs naturally do. The unlucky ones, the ones in the road, ran on and on. After a while we stopped seeing the long-haired dog, as we knew we would. It is hard to say exactly when he faded from sight. Or it may be, knowing how it had to end, we just stopped looking for him.

●

It was several months later, in late fall 2017, when he reappeared, though at first I didn't know it was even the same dog. He was about one hundred yards from the back porch, along the ridgeline, too far to see clearly in the gray mist, black trees, and thick briars, and too close to ignore. He lay completely still, his head up. He wasn't hurting anything up there, so we let him be.

The next day he was still there, in the same place. He appeared not to have moved at all. I thought Skinny, fiercely territorial, would run him off sooner or later, but she left him alone, as if she understood what was happening even if we did not. Surely, in the morning, he would be gone.

But nothing had changed, as if someone had sawn the rough shape of a dog out of an old sheet of plywood and propped it against a tree. I wondered, looking up at him, if he just wanted to be close to a house, to people, just something familiar. Like Sam, I believe a cast-off dog does not easily forget the life it had before. We wondered, my brother and me, if he went up there to die.

"Best to leave it alone," Sam told me, not unkind, just trying to lend me some common sense. He rarely had an impetuous, reckless thought, which made him a curiosity in our family. I often think we had different daddies.

We are not usually wise, in my family, not careful. When my daddy died, in my first year of high school, he left me a clip-on tie and a pair of dice. I realize, now, it was his retirement plan.

My little brother, Mark, once believed he could drive his Ford Bronco across a railroad trestle. "I thought I could do it," he said, from the bottom of the ravine.

Whole lives have passed in this way, in an absence of reason, logic, and responsibility. There are only consequences, bail, fines, and doctors, and a sad, perverse kind of pride.

"When I die, and I'm layin' there in my casket, slip me a pack of Camels in my shirt pocket," my little brother told me. "I won't need no lighter."

Getting old, I was disappointed to discover, had not made me one bit smarter.

I pulled on my boots and old duck hunting coat, and I staggered up the hill.

•

I made it only a few steps, crashing and sliding and cussing through the mud, leaves, and brush, when he vanished. He must have slipped over the ridgeline while I was busy falling down.

I found myself a tree to prop against, and sat down in the wet leaves. It had been a long time since I sat in the woods by myself, in the cold. The old duck hunter's coat was so big it was almost a shed, and it kept me warm and dry. I thought I might rest awhile. I was daydreaming about the last time I wore that coat, in a Yankee winter in Cambridge, Massachusetts, in 1993. I had never seen real winter, so heinous the Charles River froze and cars parked at the curb were buried in ice, and . . . and then I saw him, almost close enough to touch, in the corner of my right eye.

I jumped. The dog staggered back but,

surprisingly, did not run away. I knew at a glance he was no threat. He was not crazy sick, run over, or crippled or any of the things that make a dog unpredictable or dangerous; he was just done, finished, the way a beatdown boxer is done when his arms fall to his sides and he can't summon the will to cover his face.

Long-haired dogs hide their suffering better, but he seemed wired together out of hair and teeth and bones, like something you would pay a quarter to see behind glass at some Florida highway attraction in the days before Disney. His legs and belly were black with mud and his coat was tangled and matted with trash, and you could almost count the bones in his face. Blood showed in his fur in thin, watery lines. It struck me, then, it was the same dog, or what was left of it.

He had dwindled, and any menace in him had leached away, like someone had pulled a stopper and let it all run out. I guess I should have been more careful around a dog like this, but I sat back down in the leaves and reached out, slowly, so I wouldn't scare him. I scratched one ragged ear, and he licked my hand. Maybe it would have been different if he wasn't so used up. He even had trouble holding his head up. It wobbled like an old drunk's.

"You had a damned hard ol' time of it," I said, "didn't you, buddy?"

I put a slice of bread on the ground in front of him, wondering if he was even able to eat, and he ate it in two bites, then wolfed down six more as fast as I could deal them out. He gagged, a little, and coughed, but looked to me for more. He took the last slice from my hand, before I could put it down. I guess all he needed to rediscover a will to live was a half loaf of stale raisin bread.

Then he laid his head against my leg and looked at me, like he was just another lapdog that slipped the leash in a cul-de-sac and straggled home for Gravy Train. He smelled awful, but I petted him anyway, and when I stopped, he nudged at my leg till I started again, as if, having found some hint of how things used to be, he was determined not to lose that connection ever again.

That was when I noticed the eye. I tried, as gently as I could, to tap the air just above it with a fingertip. He would have blinked or shied away if there was good sight in it, but I kept at it, willing it to see. Finally, there seemed to be a slight blink. He had some sight there, but not much.

From where we sat, I could see what he had been watching. I could see the cabin, the cedar beams faded to gray now, smoke rising from the chimney and mixing in the haze along the ridge. The front yard sloped to a log fence and then to forty acres of pasture, dotted with islands of water oaks and lightning-blasted pines, and a maze of privets, blackberry bushes, and wild plums so thick the fat rabbits had to squeeze inside. The squirrels—squirrels beyond counting—ran along the wood fence, scurried across the roof of the cabin, and bolted across the ground, till the hound Skinny spotted them and sent them scrambling back into the thick trees. Pup, the small, fearful dog who was terrified of squirrels, rabbits, and most other living things, hovered near the kitchen door, where biscuits took wing twice a day and an old woman brought out heaping plates of leftover people food. It was a good place to be a dog.

"Come on," I told him, "let's go to the house."

I started down, thinking that falling down a hill would hurt more than falling up one. The dog stuck so close to my side it made it hard to walk. I stumbled over him, once, twice, then just picked him up and carried him. It was like toting a pillowcase full of sticks.

I know there was no magic in it; it was the food that won him over. I know he would have stuck fast to the side of the most miserable dog beater in north Alabama if that meant he would get fed every day or even every other day. It was no more complicated or mysterious than that.

I figured it would probably turn out badly. But I knew, as I staggered down that hill with that awful dog, what the unreliable men in my family have always known: that this ol' life can be a bleak, sorry, boring slog, if you take the time, at every turn, to think it through.

THREE

Tough Guys

THE DOG lay in the garage as I cleaned off the mud and old blood with a rag. He looked like someone had been at him with an ice pick and a dull plastic razor, and he was covered in cuts, scratches, and punctures. He had a sore, chewed-on back leg, an ugly cut or tear on his mouth, and he jumped when I touched a sore place on his ribs on the right side. But the bleeding had mostly stopped and there was no life-threatening wound that I could see. I am certainly no vet, but as a boy we were always doctoring somebody's throwaway dog. I pretty much soaked him in antiseptic and I know it stung, but he endured it, trusting, like he had always been my dog.

It was clear what had happened. A stronger,

fiercer dog, or the pack itself, had torn him up and driven him away, and he had starved. I told him over and over that he was a good boy, and I wondered how long it had been since he heard it, since he heard a human voice this way. People cussed stray dogs, and even shot at them to run them off. But he had been someone's pet once, or farm dog, or just a scruffy yard dog. Maybe he remembered that, or maybe he was just broken.

All I could do was feed him and give him a place to get better. Then, if he stayed, I would take him to the vet in Jacksonville and have him tested for heartworms, tick-borne disease, and other problems; strays lived with time bombs inside them, and it was premature to think I had saved him from anything till we knew. In the meantime, I cut some of the matted hair away, and cleaned out cockleburs, sweet-gum burs, and blackberry stickers. From a sore place on his belly, I picked out what seemed to be a rusty BB or bird shot; no telling how long he had carried that around.

It occurred to me that I didn't know how old he was. His teeth were good, a young dog's teeth; I thought he was three, four at the most, but it was hard to tell in the shape he was in. A wiser person would have put him in a pen or crate, then formed an intelligent plan on what to do when he got his strength back. But I thought a cage would terrify him. He had been wild too long.

Skinny finally took an interest. She floated up to make sure he was still not a threat, and growled just enough to get his attention. A weak, sick dog on the floor had no significance to her, and she trotted away. But she never let him out of her sight. She was smart like that.

I got him a bowl of water and he drank till I was afraid he might hurt himself. Then I gave him a big bowl of dried food, the kind dogs actually seemed to eat, but my mother sniffed and said no dog could ever get healthy again on such a dry, rattling mess as that. She did not believe in dog food squeezed out of machines and sold in fifty-pound bags. It didn't even smell like food, she said, so she made him a big skillet of milk gravy rich in bacon grease. The dog ate it all, a quart or so, and licked the bowl, then wobbled to the dried food, sniffed it, and ate that, too.

She did not question if I was right to bring him here. He was hurt and starved and could not go one step farther, so he could stay, unless he was just too dangerous to have on the place. No dog, once given asylum, had ever been chased away, but most of those dogs had the intelligence to know they had been saved. It may not make much sense, to take in only the weakest and sickest stray dogs and leave the rest of them to perish, but in a way those dogs made the decision for us.

I sat out there a long time, petting him. Something was off, but I couldn't figure out what it was. Then it struck me. The dog had not made a sound of any kind. He had not barked, whined, or whimpered. He just looked at me, and I wondered if he had been hurt so badly in his throat or neck he was mute. When I stopped petting him, he staggered up and followed me to the kitchen door, till I relented and went back with him to the garage, where he went to sleep on my foot.

My brother, sister-in-law Teresa, and her brother, Todd, came to eat supper that night, like they do most nights. My mother's kitchen is the center of the universe here.

"That's him," my brother said, looking down on the dog. "I didn't know it was him."

I do not think I have ever used the word "aghast," but that was what he was.

"I know," I said, "but you wouldn't believe . . ."

He just shook his head.

"I know," I said, "but it's like he ain't even the same dog."

The dog lay with his head on his paws, as if in prayer.

"He's bein' good," I said, and suddenly it all made me mad. I could keep the damn dog if I wanted to, but there is a dynamic between brothers that endures across the decades. He thought he was always, always right; he wasn't, but for some ridiculous reason I gave a damn what he thought.

The dog was just weak, sick, he said. This was a lull, he cautioned, nothing more.

"You need to run him off. Save yourself some bad trouble."

"I can't," I said.

"Okay," he said, talking to me the way he did when I was four or five years old, "but if he fights with Skinny, don't get between 'em."

"He's all fought out," I said.

"He won't be in his right mind, he gets to fightin'. Dogs like that, they fight to hurt."

"I think he's all right," I said. "I think he's just a lost dog."

He shrugged. It would be worth it, me getting bit, if he could be right again.

"I just don't see why you even want him."

"I don't know, either," I said, and thought, *Yeah, I do.*

He was a tough guy, knocked down.

"You got Skinny," my brother said.

"Skinny is a child of God," I said, quoting my mother, who talked pretty that way. Skinny was almost a person, an independent creature. You don't own a dog like that. You live beside it.

"You got Pup," he said.

"Pup is dumb as a sack of lead sinkers," I said, "bless his heart."

Puppy was, in that moment, peeking cowardly from the edge of the garage. He had a pronounced overbite, which made him look like he was always gritting his teeth.

"Well," my brother said, "just don't let that dog knock Momma down."

I knew he'd play that hole card sooner or later. We spent our adult lives trying to keep anything from knocking her down. I knew, if he did knock her down, or bite her, I would have to flee to Argentina on a tramp steamer, undergo backroom plastic surgery, and change my name to Alejandro.

"Don't knock Momma down," I said to the dog.

I stayed out there till after two o'clock in the morning, still a long way from my bedtime. The dog was breathing easy and eating and drinking, which was more than I expected. In the morning, if he needed a vet right away, I would take him; at least, I thought, I could feed him until he got his strength back, and give him some kind of chance, even if he decided to just walk away.

I would *not* take him to the county animal shelter—an overburdened kill shelter, doing its best—in the sorry shape he was in; I was afraid they would put him down, immediately.

He got to his feet, once, and stood weakly in the driveway. He seemed to be waiting for something. He finally barked, hoarsely, one time, when the wind carried something to him, a scent or sound, and I wondered if the strays were out there, beyond the fence.

A soft guy wouldn't have made it, I thought to myself. He was not a crazed pit bull, robot Doberman, or a Rottweiler with chronic halitosis and a bad attitude, just one awful, sin-eater of a dog. Right before I went in the house, Skinny glided into the garage and, like a monkey, leapt from box to crate to table and finally to the seat of the tractor, where she curled, looking down on him. I would not have been surprised if, one day, she just trotted up to me and actually started to talk.

I petted her head and she looked at me, questioning. She had gold-colored eyes, smarter than some people I know. *So, what are we supposed to do with this trash?* Found dogs are like that. They forget they used to be strays.

Skinny was almost dead when she showed up here about five years ago, a living skeleton. She was a mix of redbone, foxhound, and what seemed to be greyhound; she moved so lightly it seemed she had hollow bones, like a bird. When wild dogs or coyotes threatened the animals here, she fought them fearlessly, ran them off, and trailed them for miles, to make sure. Some nights, she would travel to the far corner of the land to my little brother's place. She had learned to open the door herself. She would sleep there till dawn, then come loping home for breakfast at my mother's house. My mother said she understood that my little brother needed looking after, too. Skinny had given birth to a litter of pups before she got here, but I don't know what happened to them. I doubt she abandoned them; she looked over everybody, even the hapless, quivering Puppy.

He was a grown dog now, here five years at least, the whole time with a rubber ball in his mouth. He loved to play fetch, but never figured out that, first, he had to spit it out. He ran up to us excited, expectant, then just got confused. We had to run him down and pry it out of his jaws to throw it. But you had to be careful; if you threw it into the creeping vines he would almost hang himself. Skinny would sit serenely and watch him flail, like she was watching a cartoon. Pup was frightened of *everything,* even a waving sunflower, and had to be won over again every day, like every morning was the first morning we all met. Every few months I tried to put a collar on him, and every time he tried to eat my face. I felt sorry for him, because that was all the name he had, so I attached "McGraw" to it, after the old cartoon *Quick Draw McGraw.* Puppy McGraw. It sings.

One more terribly damaged dog, I figured, would be no trouble at all.

•

For a week or so, the new dog rested, healed, and ate everything my mother put in front of him. He ate leftover beef roast, bacon, hog jowl, and pork chops with the bone cut out. He ate short ribs, and hamburger. He could eat six hot dogs, and whine for more. But he also ate butter beans, English peas, and baked sweet potatoes, and cold biscuits as fast as we could throw them into his mouth. He ate pounds of cornbread, catfish, potato salad, and pinto beans. He ate collard greens, stewed squash, and fried okra. My mother picked roast chicken off the bone for him, and cooked him scrambled eggs. She fed him sausage biscuits, and a plate of deviled eggs; I'd had my eye on those eggs all day. He lapped up milk and buttermilk, and chicken noodle soup.

I told her that this much people food was

probably bad for him—for any of us, most likely—and she lied and said she wouldn't, anymore. I watched him chew on a hambone the size of a balled-up fist, till it just disappeared. He was not fond of onions, unless battered and fried, or cucumbers or pickles of any kind, unless in a cheeseburger, but that was the litany of things he would not consume. He wore chili in his whiskers, and hush puppies on his breath.

You could almost see him heal, like some kind of time-lapse photography. By the second week, he was ranging, a little stiff legged, around the yard. One day, in his second week, he limped over to watch the donkeys, Buck and Mimi, and the great mule, Bella, as they ate from the trough by the upper-pasture gate; he seemed fascinated by them. *Livestock.* It was like he knew they had something to do with him, somehow, if he could just remember what that used to be. He eventually left his place in the garage and lay, instead, just outside the gate, so he could see them better, as if he was on some kind of mission. But he never bothered them, just seemed to study them, in a way.

I surprised myself, those days, at how much of my time that dog soaked up. I always worked in manic spurts and lately I had worked twenty-hour days, seven days a week. I didn't have time to fool with a dog. A lifetime ago I had been one of those little boys who would run around all day with a broken bird in a shoebox, expecting a miracle. Then, when all hope was lost, I buried it in the yard with a tablespoon. Not much use for a boy like that, for such a long, long time.

Now, every time I walked through the door he was waiting for me, and made every step I made. He was gentle with my mother, never jumping on her or begging for food, even if she had bacon in her hands. It was as if the dog that ran and fought in the ditches had washed away on that ridge.

"Why, he's a big baby," my mother said, rubbing his head.

His tail wagged so hard it moved his whole backbone.

"Let me see if I can find you some bologna."

FOUR

Pandemonium

I WOKE UP to shrieking.
    Dogs, mules, cats, all.
    A donkey screamed.
An old woman cursed.
A smart dog snarled in rage.
A small dog yelped in terror.
A bad dog howled in joy.
A mule kicked a metal gate, again and again.
Boom!
Boom!
Boom!
I threw off the covers, and ran.
A cat clung to the screen door, five feet up,
hissing.
I swung it, cat and all, wide open.
And saw bedlam.

Havoc.

Pandemonium.

I rushed out, barefoot, into the end of times.

And it had been going so well.

•

"RICKY!"

"RICKY!"

"RICKY!"

I made it to the porch, to see an octogenarian beating my dog with a broken broom handle.

"He's killin' my Puppy!" she screamed.

The new dog had the Puppy's neck in his jaws, growling. I saw Skinny, like a missile, streak from the hillside, and sink her teeth into one of the new dog's back legs.

The Puppy wailed. Skinny dug her feet in the dirt and pulled. Cats ran in every direction, spitting, literally climbing the cedar walls of the house and the screens on the windows and doors, all the way to the rooftop. The livestock thundered up to the side gate, to see what the excitement was about, and I guess just to lose their collective minds. The big mule liked to kick the gate when it was hungry or petulant or mad or scared, and now it hammered it, again and again and . . .

My sweet mother teed up on the speckled dog, and swung away.

Smack.

"I will KILL you!"

Smack.

"I will beat you to death . . ."

Smack.

". . . you little . . ."

Smack.

". . . SB!"

If Bigfoot had skipped across the yard in a porkpie hat, it would have been less surprising to me than my sweet, elderly mother dog-cussing a . . . well, a dog, and I wondered if I might still be asleep, dreaming. The dog ignored her, the beating, all of it. I do not think he even felt it.

I hurried down the steps, took a good running start, and, as much as I hated to do it, kicked him in the side with my bare foot to try to get him to turn loose of the smaller dog.

He let go, but turned on Skinny, teeth gnashing. I grabbed his collar and a handful of fur and tried to drag him away. He bit me, not good, but he got me, but I got my knee between him and Skinny. Then Skinny bit me, too. She wasn't herself. And I guess I'd been warned.

Puppy, the only dog that had not bit me yet,

lost what was left of his mind and ran in circles, snapping at the air. I grabbed the broom handle and was preparing to smack my own rescued dog when the dogs broke apart, snarling. I got between them with the broom handle, yelling at Skinny to git; of the two of them, I figured she had the most sense. She finally seemed to hear me and trotted off, leaving the new dog with no one to bite but me.

My mother, still scared and mad, reclaimed her broom handle and walked toward him to administer one more lick, for Jesus, I suppose. He just sat down, and wagged his tail.

She froze, the stick held over her head like a sword.

"What's wrong?" I asked.

"I can't beat a dog while it's sittin' down," she said, but I don't think she had ever beaten one while it was standing up, either.

The dog was, suddenly, an angel, glued to my leg, as if none of this had even happened; more likely, it was just that it was of no importance to him anymore.

"Bad dog!" I said, uselessly.

"I got him three or four good licks," she said.

"I know," I said.

"I don't think I hurt him," she said. "I don't think

he even knew I was beatin' him. It never fazed him."

"I thought I heard somebody cussing," I said as I tried to get my breath.

"No," she said.

"Seemed like it," I said.

"No," she said.

She considered, for a moment, the hazard of compounding her sin of cussing with that of lying.

"I might have called him an SB," she said.

The dog wagged his tail, happy to be the center of attention, again.

"He's got a demon in him," she said.

She mumbled to herself for a long while, about how it would be a cold day in hell before he got any more scraps. She told him she would put him on the road, and call the animal control, or put him in jail for life, and then she turned her back and stomped in the house, taking the stick with her.

The Puppy was catatonic, but when I finally got close enough to look at his neck I found he had not a mark on him. The new dog had only clamped down and growled.

But he was not done. I heard the donkeys screaming like they were being slaughtered and found the dog nipping at their heels in a blur of kicking and stomping. Buck sprang into the air and came down on him with all four feet bunched together like a rodeo bronc; it is how they killed coyotes. Then Mimi ran over him like a taxicab. He rose from the dust and pushed them into a screaming run. I just watched; there's not much a man on foot can do with a stampede.

"You have lost your damn mind," I said, for the first of what would turn out to be a million times, as he raced back into the yard. "Are you trying to kill your stupid self?"

But the only one injured in any of this hysteria was me. I had two minor dog bites and a knot on the top of my foot. That afternoon, I was hunched over my leg with a bottle of peroxide.

"I guess he got his strength back," my brother said.

I wondered if I needed a shot of penicillin.

"It is hard being right," he told me, "all the time."

•

That evening I took the dog his supper in jail.

"What the hell were you thinkin'?"

He just looked at me.

"Nothin'," I said. "That's what I thought."

He reared up on his hind legs like a boxing kangaroo.

"For God's sake," I said, and let him out, again. He was good for about ten minutes, then repaid me for letting him out by sneaking off to pick another fight with the five-hundred-pound mule.

I had stupidly hoped that being here, being part of the place, would gentle him, somehow. He did not have to fight for food; there was an excess of it. I hoped he would realize he no longer had to fight for dominance. The only female was spayed. I guess I just didn't think it through.

Skinny had been the clear alpha here, and I guess he couldn't stand that. Every night, for weeks, there was one quick, loud fight, over nothing at all. Skinny was lighter than him, but fighting her was like fighting a weed eater. They fought for just a few loud, ugly seconds, then, without having hurt each other at all, broke apart, growling. The only other dog was a brain-addled coward. The new dog seemed to realize this, and so decided to torture him, for the fun of it.

The dogs got table scraps throughout the day, but after dark they got a big scoop of dry dog food. Speck routinely ran the smaller dog away from his bowl, took a single bite, and just lay there, to prevent the Puppy from eating. If the Puppy went to the other bowl, the new dog got up and lay down in that one, and kept moving between the two, till he had eaten it all, or the Pup, thoroughly confused, just gave up. We had to hand feed him, or lock the new dog in jail; leading him away from the Pup's supper, or even kicking him away, only worked till we turned our back.

"You can't have both bowls," I told the new dog.

Yes, I can.

"You can't starve the Puppy. Momma likes the Puppy. We all like the Puppy."

Skinny did not suffer his foolishness. If he came close to her bowl she bit.

He seemed jealous of every bit of attention we showed the other dogs. He had watched as we threw balls for the Pup, and one night he rushed in to play. But he could not easily follow the trajectory of the ball. So, in pure devilment, he started stealing the balls from Pup and hoarding them. Every time he stole a ball, he buried it. I had to get the Pup another, to stop him from going altogether catatonic, till the dog stole it, too; it was a treadmill of hopelessness, $3.99 at a time.

"You ought to be ashamed of yourself," I said.

He gnawed on a hard rubber ball, unconcerned.

"Bad dog!" I said.

He rolled over on his back in the middle of his

bounty of rubber balls, and grinned at me, upside down. And it occurred to me I had rescued the dog just to turn him loose in a dangerous place, a place that might have been paradise for a well-behaved dog but was a minefield for a badly behaved, one-eyed one. I was less afraid he would kill himself than blind himself as he ran through blackberry thickets, briars and brush, and the barbed wire that lined miles of the place. It became almost a ritual, every night when he came crashing down the ridge to see me: I checked his eyes.

He made of himself such a constant pain that, every night, he had to be dragged off to the slam. Oddly, he seemed content to be locked up at the end of every day, or at least resigned. I believe, in time, the dog did not see the pen as punishment at all, just another place to eat his supper.

"He is good about going to jail," my brother acknowledged.

I never, not once, considered getting rid of him.

I can live with a lot on my conscience, but not that.

A few months later, a photographer came to do a story here, and Speck tried to mate with him. But the photographer was kind, and attempted to gently extract himself.

"What a beautiful animal," he said.

I led Speck off to jail, muttering.

My brother saw him there as he drove in.

"What'd he do?" he asked. It had become what we said to each other, instead of "hello."

"Tried to have relations with a photographer," I said.

"Well," he said.

Speck barked, once, to let me know it was time for a jailbreak. I let him out, then trudged tiredly back to the house.

"The photographer called him a 'beautiful animal,'" I told my brother. As we watched, leaning on the pickup, he assaulted a calico tomcat. I don't know why.

"A 'beautiful animal,'" I said.

"Oh, yeah," he said.

He was still nameless. I tried on a few, but they didn't sing. I thought about Rip, and Booger, and Festus. I considered Muddy, for Muddy Waters, and Hank, and Merle. I thought about Neckbone, and Streak, from a James Lee Burke novel, and Bruiser, from Grisham's *The Rainmaker.* I thought about Dodger, from Dickens, from the way he darted in and out of the stampede. I considered Opie, or Ope, for short, and Pine Knot, and then I just gave up. Give a dog time, the old people said, and he will name himself.

•

The holidays came and went. He was *not* good, but on Christmas he got a hambone, an economy-sized box of Greenies, and a pan of cornbread dressing—and a bag of tiny dog treats that he did not seem to appreciate. For a dog spoiled as badly as him, it was like feeding him a Tic Tac.

He seemed healthy, but as the New Year came and winter began to fade I knew I could not put off taking him to the vet any longer. I hung a leash on a nail in the garage, for the next morning, hoping he would not go crazy when I put it on; I considered putting it on him the evening before, just to let him get used to it, but I was afraid if it went badly he might run when he saw it again. I figured that getting bit once was better than getting bit twice; there didn't seem to be much sense in practicing it.

He was still just a few months from living wild, and I had seen him in the pasture, nudging closer to the road, listening to the strays in the distance.

In a ragged way, white-trash kind of way, it reminded me of the great dog Buck in London's *Call of the Wild.*

. . . he sprang from sleep with a start . . . From the forest came the call . . . And he knew it, in

the old familiar way . . . and he was haunted by
recollections . . .

But he would always turn away and rush back
up the hill, clomp up the porch steps and wait
for his snack, and take a nap on my foot. I put a
glow-in-the-dark collar on him, with my name and
phone number written on it, in case he should
wander off, but I think he knew he was home.

The next morning, he was gone.

{ FIVE }

Geraldine

I WALKED FOR MILES, calling that stupid dog.
I tried to whistle, but I never could whistle a
lick. I guess it must have looked pretty sad,
a grown man whistling without sound, trying to
call in a dog with no name. I checked the ridge
where I found him, then walked miles of fence,
acres of woods. When it was finally clear that he
was just gone, I started driving, from Cove Road to
Carpenters Lane, Old Tredegar Church to Pleasant
Valley, Green's store to the chert pits on Nisbet
Lake Road. I idled along Hulsey Road and went
north to Blue Hole, to the illegal dumps where old
mattresses and refrigerators went to die. I bounced
over pulpwood trails and powerline roads, past
trailer parks and boarded-up houses and every
desolate patch of red mud for fifteen miles.

I searched till after one in the morning, till I was beginning to weave into the ditches and scare myself awake. Back in the yard I sat in a chair under the outside light and threw the ball for Puppy, who tracked it down by moonlight. Skinny trotted up and sat beside me; I guess it was the most peaceful night either of them had enjoyed in quite some time. Like some little kid, I finally went inside and tried to sleep, thinking that my bad dog would be there when I woke up, that I would hear that usual melee in the yard, and there he would be, unkempt, guilty, and unashamed.

I drove for two days, thinking my phone would ring and it would be someone who just found him, wandering. I decided to do what every boy did when he lost a dog. I would staple flyers on telephone poles and put an alert on the Internet. Then I climbed into my truck for one more aimless search. I pulled to the end of the drive and stopped, trying to decide which way to go. I guess it didn't matter. He was just gone, just a road dog after all.

•

He made it as far as the driveway before he gave out. I saw him there as I turned in off the main road that afternoon, just a few feet from the mailbox. He was lying on his side, next to a little puddle of blood. I thought he might be dead.

"Hey, buddy," I said, and he raised his head and thumped his tail on the asphalt one weak time.

I was afraid to handle him, at first, in case he had been hit by a car and was broken up inside, but it only took a minute to see that he had lost another dogfight. Both ears were bleeding where they joined the skull, as if something had tried to rip them off; both inner ears were caked with blood and infection. His throat had a wound in it, and his breathing had an odd, hoarse whistle. The back of his neck was spongy from bites, and his thick fur was soaked with blood; all his wounds were infected; you could smell the decay on him.

His right leg, a different one this time, was lame and still trickling blood. And he still didn't whine, didn't make a sound. What calamity did it take to make this dog do that? I got an old quilt from inside, scooped him up, and carried him into the garage, then went inside to call the vet.

I stepped back outside to see my mother stooped over the dog, speaking softly but earnestly to him like he was a human child. The dog had his head turned to her and seemed to be listening to every word.

". . . so we'll name you after one of our Georgia cousins, Geraldine. She was my aunt Louvadie's adopted granddaughter. Aunt Louvadie adopted her mother, Bell, and Bell had Geraldine and Gerry Bob. They all lived over in Georgia before they came to Alabama, in about '51. Geraldine had black hair and big, big freckles, more freckles than you have ever seen in your life, freckles just like you got. Geraldine always wanted to go to Hollywood, not to be in the movies, just to live in Hollywood. She loved the movie stars. Nobody in particular; she just loved the whole *set*. She had pictures of movie stars taped all over her mirror. And she did go to Hollywood, too . . . we got a postcard from Geraldine from Hollywood. It just said: 'I made it. Ha-Ha.' And she never come back home . . . But anyway, none of that has nothing to do with you.

"When Geraldine was still just a little girl, she come to our house with Louvadie . . . and Daddy saw all them freckles, just hundreds and hundreds and hundreds of 'em, and he named her right then and there. He said, 'Why, she's a speckled beauty.' I guess he wanted to make her feel better, you know, about being homely. And that's what we'll call you. But not 'cause you're ugly, but 'cause of all your freckles. We'll call you the Speckled Beauty."

I came out and lifted him up.

"I named him," she said.

"I heard," I said.

"He'll be all right," she said. My people think a good story will fix just about anything. I made her promise to tell me the whole story again, when we got back. I lifted him into the back seat of my pickup, and must have hurt him a little because he nipped my hand; he had hurt me worse snatching a table scrap.

They took him straight into the back when I carried him in, as I did the paperwork at the front desk.

"What's his name?" the receptionist asked.

I knew I did not have time to go into the odyssey of Geraldine Thomason Bundrum.

"His name is Speck," I said.

•

They glued him back together. There was no long-term damage to the wounded leg or the neck or throat or ears. His repaired left ear kind of jutted out at an odd angle, like he was signaling a left turn, but the truth is I could not remember if it looked that way before. I did not want the vet to think I was ungrateful; I would hate to have to glue an ear in place and get it straight. More important, his blood test showed he was free of disease or parasites; for a dog that had run wild for so long, that, alone, was a small miracle.

But the vet told me that what had happened would likely happen again, and again, unless we had him neutered. I had considered this, and dreaded it, and I guess I cowardly hoped I could just put it off forever. But I knew he was right, especially in this dog's case. I did not know why he ran off, whether it was to run after a female in heat, or just to rejoin a pack. But he had been wild a long time. He liked to fight, and liked to wander, and if I wanted him to survive his nature, I should have the operation done right away. Then, with any luck at all, he could live a long, easy life.

I would not have done it, whether it was the right or responsible thing or not, just to have a dog. But this really did seem to be a choice between life and a suffering, violent death. He might not have a chance, might be a stray at his core, and would, once healthy, run off, anyway.

I had Skinny spayed years before, believing it was the best thing in the long run for her health. I planned to have Puppy neutered, too, but he seemed frozen in second grade, and had shown no interest in females or in traveling, and he was older than Speck. Plus, he bit me when I tried to load him in the car, and he bit like he meant it. He was so slobbering, wild-eyed scared when we tried to handle him that he forgot to breathe, so we eventually just put it off, indefinitely.

Speck had proved he would not last. He might see this as home, but he would always be drawn away. The vet said it would be a good time to do it, now, in the lull caused by these other injuries, rather than wait for the next catastrophe, the next bad fight that he couldn't win.

I told the vet to go ahead. I left him there, but as I drove home I knew it was an impossible choice. The dog did not want a long, easy life, and I elected to give it to him, anyway.

•

He stayed three days, healing from the surgery and his various wounds. He conned the nice people there, too; they gave him pets, treats, and called him handsome. But he was ready to go when he heard my voice in the lobby, and came rushing out in that frantic way dogs do when they hear their person close by. On the way home I went by the Sonic and got him two chili dogs, though I guess one of them was for me. But he eyed the other one with such avarice that I gave it to him, too. I know

that smart people will say that chili is a terrible
thing for a dog to eat, but maybe not so much after
a year or two eating used paper towels, eggshells,
and an occasional gopher snake.

"What do you think of your name," I asked him
as I wiped chili off the leather seat.

Nothing.

"I know what you're thinking. You're thinking
that 'the Speckled Beauty' sounds like a girl's
name, but it's not. It's a pretty snazzy name, when
you think about it."

Nothing.

"Well, you don't have to get all snooty about it.
She could have named you Geraldine."

•

The vet said it would take him awhile to gentle,
maybe months before he became less aggressive,
less destructive, less likely to wander. It depended
on the dog, but two months, usually, was the
telltale point, and I could not help but wonder how
much of my terrible dog had survived.

He didn't know what had happened to him, of
course. He had always been glued to me, since the
start; it was a condition of the breed. And again,
he sat with me on the porch for hours, listening

to me talk without saying a damn thing, till he heard or sniffed or sensed an intruder in the dark. Then he sprang to it . . . or tried to. He was still sore, still gimpy, and he flew just halfway up the hill before he came limping back. He was there, in spirit, but the rest of him was all stitched up.

"I'm sorry, buddy," I told him.

He couldn't answer, of course. But he just squeezed his head under my arm, and leaned, as if he was trying to.

It's okay.

SIX

Jackasses

ABOUT TWO MONTHS LATER, the dog considered the mule through the wire, not growling or snapping, just looking. It was a little sad, at first. His wounds and his surgery were healed, though he was still a little sore. I guess he had gentled, changed. That dog had not been afraid of anything.

I should have known better. He was not misbehaving, but he was *thinking* about it.

It started with a low, soft growl, so faint I could barely hear it, but he held that sinister note for a long time.

Grrrrrrrrrrrrrrrrrrrrrrrrrrrrr.

Then he howled like some kind of demon dog and launched himself at the barbed wire. He ducked at the last second, scraping a handful of fur off his back, and the wire twanged like a guitar string.

He leapt straight at the big mule's nose, driving her backward, then circled around and nipped at her heels.

I watched, helpless, as she did that odd hitch-step that mules do, like they are coiling a spring, or cocking a gun, and kicked him square in his chest with both her hind legs.

She must have pulled it at the last second, because otherwise she would have crushed him, but it was force enough to send him flying backward through the air. He did not fly far, just a few feet. It was the juxtaposition, not the distance, that was remarkable.

There he went, tailfirst.

Zoom.

Now that, I remember thinking as I ran as fast as I was able to see if he was all right, *is something you don't see every day.*

He landed on his feet, roaring, sliding, his claws digging into gravel, and rushed back through the wire, I guess because being kicked ten feet or so was not quite scary enough.

In seconds, he had succeeded in bunching all three jackasses together against the heavy pasture gate and barbed wire and was lunging and snarling as the mule and donkeys all tried to stomp and kick him. The air filled with dust, and the gate trembled on its hinges as the mule and donkeys smashed into it again and again, the dog dancing out of the way in time to avoid being mashed to pulp there, too. A stranger to this little asylum would have thought my dog, surely, had gone bug-eyed crazy, but what he really was, in that moment of pure, perfect chaos, was happy.

I didn't have much time to think about it. I cussed the jackasses and all jackasses before them, unhooked the gate with a pure dread, and waded into the melee on the other side, to see if my bad dog, apparently unaffected by science, surgery, or even prayer, could get me killed, once more. I grabbed his collar and dragged him to the gate, his toenails digging in the gravel like hooks.

My mother came to the porch, wringing her hands.

"What in the world . . ."

"Jackasses!" I hollered, to the sky, and she told me to watch my language.

"Jackasses, jackasses, jackasses," I said, almost singing it. "We are covered up in #!$%*##*%!!!*)~)&# *jackasses! That . . . is . . . what . . . is . . . wrong!"* I think I might have done a little dance.

The dog, thinking this was some kind of exhortation, broke loose and rushed into the pasture again, and because I am as damaged as he is, I waded in with him. I have a phobia about jackasses stepping on my feet, and I did a ridiculous, old-man shimmy as I tried to evade them, to try to save his life. The mule shied away from me and ran. But I was so distracted I forgot to watch for the remaining threat, and Buck kicked me so hard in my left hip I couldn't feel my leg.

I used language you usually only hear on Cinemax.

The dog trotted at my side, overjoyed, as I limped to the house.

We showed them, huh?

"Yeah," I said, "we showed them."

The mule—and, in a lesser way, the donkeys—would remain his primary nemesis, and in a way, I believe, just the fight he needed. For months, I had worried if he would still have the big life he had before. I pictured a sedate, lazy lump, shuffling around the place: I imagined that good dog, I suppose. But if I had any lingering fear that he was going soft, he erased it in the pounding hoofbeats, rising dust, and flying mud. It got so bad that the nightly dogfights, cat molestations, terrified deliverymen, and other malfeasance were little more than an intermission. I worried, once again, he would get stomped to death . . . and I never liked that damn mule, anyway.

•

I do not mind jackasses, per se.

I liked the donkeys, when they had all four feet on the ground. It is impossible to look at them and not smile. Called Sicilians, they kicked, bit, and stepped on my toes, but they were only waist high, composed of big heads, potbellies, and soft noses; my mother loved them like her children.

Before they came, the land was covered in beautiful cattle; but my mother was afraid of the bulls, of being chased as she walked to her pond to fish. And so we had the cattle moved out, and I became the jackass wrangler I am today. There is not much nobility in being a jackass man, but as much as I missed the cows, which had generated actual *income,* I was glad my mother could walk unafraid across her land. There is little resolution in a family like ours; the never-ending conflicts pile in layers, gathering frustration like old dust. But for once, just once, I won.

Then, ten years ago, I came home to see, looking at me across the wire, a great, black, satanic mule.

She was taller than me at the ears, with hooves

the size of a Quaker Oats box. When I tried to pet her she swung her hundred-pound head like an anvil at my jaw, just missing, and ran kicking, screaming in a high-pitched, nerve-shattering frequency. Only her eyes were gentle, a deep brown. But a mule has lying eyes. Ask any old man, leaning on a crutch, and he will tell you. My mother bought her from a cousin on the mule-trading Bundrum side of the family, for one hundred dollars.

"They wanted three hundred dollars," she said. "I got a *deal.*"

"Oh, yeah," I said. "But what, exactly, were you going to do with a mule? You are a little too old to plow . . ."

"I got it for your little brother," she said. "He needs a mule."

"Nobody needs a mule," I said. "What the hell is he gonna do with a mule?"

My little brother was too old to plow, too. We did not even own a plow that you didn't pull with a Kubota.

"He just needs one," she said.

It has been a decade, and he has yet to take possession of his mule. I am left with mule maintenance, for the rest of my life. They live a long, long time, and I am not feeling so good.

I had considered, briefly, being buried in the pasture, but now I cannot do that, for the thought of Bella leaving hoofprints—and much, much worse things—upon my grave.

She is not even a good mule. She is not saddle broke, so any attempt to ride her would result in certain death. Worse, you have to be constantly aware of which way she was pointed. If you walk up behind her, it might be the last thing you ever do.

Plus, she is devious. In the afternoon, when she decides she is ready to eat, she kicks the galvanized gate over and over, a hundred times. If you give in and feed her early, she will kick it in hopes, I guess, that I am soft in the head and will feed her again. Some days she would kick it when my brother, sister-in-law, or cousin Jeanette pulled up. Some days she got fed four times.

But I let her take root here, too, because I knew the real reason the old woman wanted her. She was a reminder of her past, a bridge to a harder, harsher, sweeter time.

My grandfather followed mules, cursing, staggering, across poor, rented ground. They all had names, and became part of the family. There was Lucifer, Daisy, and Buttercup, and they were the machine that fed and clothed them. If a man had a good mule, he could gouge a living out of the red dirt.

What is odd is how the rich folks seemed to love them, too. The mule endures in a strange kind of fascination for Southern intellectuals, and has even been *studied* by them. They have determined there can be no genuine Southern literature unless it has at least one mule in it, preferably a dead one. Faulkner said a mule would wait patiently a lifetime for an opportunity to kick you once, which tells me Faulkner did not know shit about mules. Mules will kick you hard and often and when it is convenient; if they only kicked once it was because they killed you the first time.

As I feared, my mother never walked in her pasture again. I spent a lifetime working to buy her a farm, a real one, only to surrender it to a murderous mule. But her heart would not allow me to get rid of it, though I doubt if I could ever find that big a fool.

•

The thing is, the mule seemed to feel the same about me. Late one night, not long after she arrived, my brother and I were in the pasture, searching for a leak in a water line. We were hunched over a muddy place in the grass when I heard a soft footstep behind my back and hot breath on my neck. I wheeled around with my flashlight and found myself nose to nose with what seemed to be a massive, mutant, bucktoothed, man-eating rabbit.

"Argh," I said.

She screamed right in my face, and for a horrifying second I thought I was about to be chomped to death by two rows of giant yellow teeth.

"It's just the mule, for God's sake," my brother said.

She ran off into the dark, kicking and screaming.

"Now you've gone and scared her," he said.

I swept the pasture with my flashlight, to make sure the mule monster was not sneaking up on me again. Of all the ways I might leave the world, being trampled by a giant mule in the dark, then finished off by a pair of miniature donkeys, is not how I would like my obituary to read. But I made up my mind, then, I would not give her the chance. I would keep my distance, till one of us was under the grass. Then the bad dog arrived.

•

"If she ever gets him good, and kills him, won't be nobody's fault but his," said my brother, after watching her punt him into the wire.

"That won't make him any less dead," I said.

The crazy dog even wanted to fight her over her food. He hunkered down across the wire from her trough, and stole mouthfuls through the strands, under her nose.

I asked learned people, farmers and vets and old people, if the horse feed would hurt him, and they said they did not know, since they had never, in all their lives, conceived of a dog that peculiar.

"You don't even like horse feed," I told him, and pushed him back with the toe of my boot.

He barked once, sharp. He only did this in disagreement.

Yes, I do.

"No, you don't."

The bark again.

Yes, I do.

•

My brother told me he might have a solution. He had used a shock collar on troublesome hunting dogs, dogs that could not be taught to mind any other way.

We could wait for my dog to chase a car, or fight the mule, or try to make love to a photographer, and zap him a time or two with the remote control.

"We can't do that," I said.

"You can set it real, real low," he said.

He called it "bumping."

"I am NOT gonna shock my dog into doin' right," I said.

"Why not?" he asked. "I don't think you can teach him any other way."

"I ain't going to electrocute my own dog," I said.

The truth is, I am afraid that once I started zapping him, I might not be able to stop.

"Just a little bit," he said, "you know, when he misbehaves."

"No," I said.

"Just a . . ."

"No."

SEVEN

Big Deal

I DON'T MEAN TO BRAG, but I'm a pretty big deal in the Huddle House.

I come here almost every day and sit by myself in a corner booth. I watch the people come in, and I nod or wave. I know most of them. Working people. Menthols in their lips.

The waitresses know my order by heart. Eggs. Grits. No toast. The doctors, while meaning well, have taken much of the joy from my life. They took my sausage, first, then my bacon, hash browns, and, finally, my toast. What kind of sadist takes a man's toast?

The waitresses have watched the joy in my life dwindle, but they are too kind to say anything. They plop down little plastic tubs of apple butter that they know I cannot eat, but they keep on plopping them down, in case I should rediscover some zest for life, or just a will to live.

I linger over my breakfast, and eavesdrop. I hear all the dirt in town and am always a little disappointed my name does not come up. My truck broke down once in front of the Gamecock Motel in 1983 and people talked bad about me for three years. But I guess old sins are all I have, anymore. So, I sit, watch the traffic in the summer heat, and wonder how it all came to this.

I was never a rich guy, but I saw more of this world than I ever thought I would. I wore out some shoe leather on the Upper West Side, and a good Ford truck on the 405. I had a shotgun double in New Orleans, a '69 Firebird in Miami, and spent four months in a hot hotel room in Port-au-Prince. I watched a camel train appear, like a mirage, on a desert horizon, walked with elephants, fished the Gulf, and damn near got eaten by an alligator on a rainy night in Belle Glade. I guess I did what I wanted most of my life. But this ol' earth must surely be round, 'cause I found myself right back where I started, in a slightly better pickup truck.

I was still a little wobbly from the chemotherapy when I showed up at my mother's cabin in 2015. I was in remission, but what lingered in me did not show in the lab work or in an MRI. The treatment muddled my thinking, confused the colors, and even burned holes in my memory. The other patients called it chemo brain, a common thing, but in the strangest way it whittled down my confidence, my arrogance, and guts. I had not known such a thing was even possible, as if someone crept into my house in the middle of the night and stole all the pictures of me, before. I can't blame chemo for it all. Stupid, the older I got, was my natural state.

I always came home, when I wasn't sure where else to go. They had to take me; my name was on the water bill. But as the months with my mom slipped by, I knew I was probably here to stay.

Her vision was almost gone, her steps were slow and careful. I needed to be here, if for no other reason than to ask, night by night, if she was all right, or needed anything, and to make sure she turned off the oven. She was glad to have me home, but insulted at the idea of her own frailty. I did not have to stay, she said. She lived most of her life alone, the rest propping up sorry men.

One day, she pulled off her hat to show me a fresh haircut. It was a little ragged.

"Who cut it?" I asked.

"Me and Jesus," she said.

Sometimes, it was hard to tell who was minding

who. She still treated me like I was a child, in a time of moon shots and tail fins.

"It's what I see," she said, when I asked her why she did that. I guess there is no place else on earth I can be.

I take a nap almost every afternoon. Yesterday, I cleaned out the feed bins, bought corn for my brother's pigs, sharpened my pocketknife, and went through my sock drawer. I found a dollar, one glove, and a cassette tape of the Charlie Daniels Band from, I think, '78. I don't know what I was saving that dollar for. I sat in my truck in the driveway and watched a red-tailed hawk hunt in the privet maze. I watched the Weather Channel, washed my truck, even wrote a word or two.

I have an old house three hundred miles from here, a mile or so from Mobile Bay. I love the water, but I haven't seen the bay, or the blue-green waters of the Gulf of Mexico, in two years. I am afraid if I leave here even for a little while, the hand of some great clock will clang into place and sweep the last of my people away. A smart aleck would say I'm half buried here, already, and as the years go by the less I give a damn. I think I always knew I'd never get out of this red dirt alive.

"Are you him?" people ask, sometimes.

"I used to be," I answer.

"I had to read your books in school," they say.

"Well," I say.

"My momma did, too," they say.

"Well."

"My grandma *loves* you."

"Tell her I said hey."

I guess there is a loneliness in it, being the sixty-year-old man who lives in his mother's basement, and I sit there sometimes in my corner booth and let the melancholy wash over me.

But it is a peaceful place, the Huddle House. Sometimes the cigarette cloud can get a little overwhelming, but this is my place, my sanctuary. They allow smoking, but not dogs.

Lately, he stuck his nose into every hole and every rotten log, almost begging to be bitten by a ground rattler or copperhead or cottonmouth. He dug nests of yellow jackets from the ground till his head swelled so badly he looked like the Elephant Man. I caught him gnawing an innocent turtle, which I rescued and carried a half mile out into the woods, intending to set it free, but the dog trailed me every step, me cussing, yelling, telling him to go to the house. But it was his damn turtle and he wanted it back. I finally gave up and locked him in jail and turned the confused turtle, a small land tortoise, loose in the grass, then went and sat on the tailgate of my truck to swing my legs and think how that was two full hours of my life that I would never get back.

But for an hour or so a day, I hide. On Tuesdays, I can even get a free pancake. I can't eat it, but I know it's out there.

My phone rang beside my sweating glass of iced tea.

"Hello," I say.

"Who is this?" my momma asks.

"It's me, Momma," I say. "You called me."

"Well, you didn't sound like yourself," she says.

"What's wrong?" I ask.

"Your dog . . ."

•

He lurked in the woods till my mother fed the cats, then swooped in.

But he didn't figure on Spew, a big, gray tom with spooky yellow eyes, who had fathered most of the cats on this place. Spew led the resistance when the dog came bounding onto the back porch and began to eat the cat food. This resulted in a cacophony of mewling, hissing, spitting, caterwauling, and, because it was cats, an inconsolable sulking. Spew stood his ground, for a little while, even took a swipe or two at the dog, and left a gash on his nose.

But the resistance, as noisy and dramatic as it was, ultimately failed, and by the time I got home the dog was sprawled as if dead, sleeping off about two pounds of Meow Mix.

"He has to go to jail," my mother said, still out of breath from trying to restore some kind of order with her broom.

"I will, in a minute," I said.

I sat down next to him on the step, kind of weary myself, and examined his nose. I was getting good at it. The dog had been here about six months, at this point, and had been cut, stung, bit, clawed, infested, infected, and choked; recently he stole a chicken thigh off the kitchen counter, but I got him in a headlock and pulled it out of his throat just as the bones began to splinter.

I thought the excitement was over this day, but I underestimated how a cat will hold a grudge.

I saw Spew a second or two before the dog did. He was slinking through the tall grass in the pasture, hunting field mice. Something made him freeze, turn, and look up the hill in our direction; then he started to yowl. I do not speak cat, but his tone, drifting up the hill, made me think he was still upset. It woke the dog, who howled like I had jabbed him with a hot coat hanger; he despised an insolent cat. He launched himself so hard off the porch he missed the last two steps, and landed hard on his chin; he sometimes misjudged his trajectory, and touchdown, on the dismount.

He was a blur by the time he hit the fence line, but again he misjudged his approach. He does not slow as he ducks under the wire and this time he hit the bottom strand so hard as he rose—too soon—that the staples pulled loose from one post. He tore up a *barbed-wire fence*. Top that.

Spew evaporated in the high grass and then magically reappeared near a tangle of rusted wire and fence posts outside an old, fallen-in log house that had been empty for 150 years. The last I saw of Speck was his tail as he dove in after him. I was not greatly concerned for the dog or the mean cat. He liked to chase cats for fun, not push them into a tight space and fight them, unless there was cat food involved; this was probably a good thing, because Spew was a straight razor, walkin'.

When he didn't quickly reappear, though, I got a little worried. Even though I knew it was useless, I tried to call him back.

"SPECK! HERE!"

Nothing.

I saw my brother's work truck limp up the drive.

"What's goin' on," he said, from the open window.

"I think one of the toms has murdered my dog," I said.

"Well," he said.

The dog reappeared a few minutes later. He was limping, and I thought maybe he had gotten bitten or scratched. But when I got him to hold still I found a rusted, two-foot strand of barbed wire stapling his tail to his right back leg. It was wound into his long hair and digging in deeper and cutting him with every step and wag of his tail. Not thinking, I grabbed the wire with both hands and tried to hold it away from his body, and managed to nick the big vein in my left wrist as the dog shied away. (It bled for an hour, and I thought, for a while, he had finally killed me.)

"Get his collar and hold him still. Don't worry about the wire," my brother said as he went to his toolbox for some clippers. Carefully, we cut it free. All we could figure was that the dog had snagged himself on an old fence outside the derelict cabin, and a piece of it had broken away.

"I mean," my brother said, holding two feet of barbed wire, "how does he even *do* stuff like this?"

The dog wagged his tail, happy, it seemed, to find it still worked properly. He was not frightened, or glum. He had tortured a stupid cat, twice, and torn up not one fence, but two; it might have been one of the greatest days of his life, and the week hadn't even gotten started good.

•

The following Friday, as we sat down for supper, my brother walked in to tell me Speck had run full speed and headfirst into the driver's side door of his red Chevy pickup as he idled up the drive; the dog hates the color red, and the shinier it is the more he hates it. We don't know why.

"Hit like a concrete block," he said as I hurried to the door, panicked.

"It's all right," he said as he and my mother followed me out. "I got out and looked. He didn't hurt it."

The dog was under my truck. It was his cave, where he went to hide from my brother, or a far-off boom of gunfire, or thunder. That is the entire litany of his fears.

"I tried to miss him," Sam said, but I knew that. He would not hurt my dog on purpose, though he did boot him off the porch every now and then. He walked back in the house, absolved. I got down on a knee and peered under the truck, so the dog could see my face.

"It's just me, buddy. You can come out now," I

said, and checked his head, back, and right side, where he was damaged before. He seemed fine, but when he appeared to be a little sluggish a few nights later I brought him in, to keep a closer watch on him.

I made a bed for him on the living room floor, but he leapt onto the old leather couch. "All right," I said, thinking this might be the safest place for him. A few minutes later I heard a small ripping sound. The leather couch was not as impervious as I had believed.

"Let's go back outside," I said, like a man who expects his dog to do what he says. He took this to mean *Catch me if you can,* and turned the living room and kitchen into a demolition derby. His paws could not get much purchase on the hardwood floor, and he slid sideways, crashing into the table, chairs, and garbage can. He nosed open a door and stumbled down the stairs and barreled into my office, turned over an iced tea, and walked through the puddle, leaving a telltale trail of paw prints that led into the bedroom. I guess I could have just followed the sounds of destruction.

By the time I got there he was eating the bed. In seconds, he had torn a hand-sized hole in an old stadium blanket I had planned, in my dotage, to drape over my cold legs; I'd had it for twenty-

five years. Then he clawed a two-foot-long scar
in the sheet and a tear in the mattress. I grabbed
his collar again, dragged him off the bed, and,
foolishly, pointed at the ripped-up mess and yelled,
"NO!" I am beginning to think that the word "no,"
in his mind, registers as, *Well, go ahead and do
whatever you want to do.* He backed straight away,
pulling, and the collar slipped over his head. I
tried to grab him by the scruff of the neck, but
he evaded me and leapt back onto the bed, and
burrowed under the blanket till he was just a big,
growling lump. He is an outside dog; he rolls
in mule manure. It wasn't that I would have to
change the bed. I might have to burn it.

He worked his head free and leered out, gleeful,
maniacal.

I slumped into my chair and laughed out loud.
I could get a new blanket, new sheet, new bed,
but the days, Lord, the days I could not change on
my own.

It was the first time I realized that the dog, more
than anything in this world, loved the sound of
people laughing. He squirmed, rolled, and, well,
grinned; I don't know what else to call it. The one
good eye lit up like neon.

"You have lost your mind," I said. I rolled him
up in it and carried him, straining, to the door, and

dumped him on the ground. He tore his way out, ripped it up, snatched it up, and ran, the sheet, in fluttering ribbons, trailing behind him like a ghost.

•

A week or so later, he attacked a car as it rolled up the drive to take me to the airport in Atlanta. Then he stared it down, nose to its bumper, his eyes locked on the driver.

"Does he bite?" the driver asked.

"He even bites me," I said.

He picked a fight with whatever the world brought him, and that day it happened to be a Lincoln. I don't think he would have hurt the driver, but he sure would have messed up a nice suit.

The next week he did it again, and the next.

My mother and I stood at the kitchen window, watching the most recent car take five minutes to traverse the last tenth of a mile, evading my dog. We had gotten over being ashamed of him twenty cars ago.

"You know why he does that," she said as I got my bag.

"'Cause he's mush headed?" I said.

"No," she said, and the *Mr. Smart Aleck* was implied. "He's figured out that when you walk out the door with a suitcase in your hand and get in a black car, you're gone a good while. He knows if you get in your truck, you come right back. You get in one of them black cars he doesn't know when you'll be back."

"I think you're overestimating how smart this dog is," I told her, and said my goodbyes and headed for the door. But I think she might have been right this time. I have heard that dogs have a faulty sense of time, but there was a difference in this dog, in how high he could jump, when I came home after a long trip.

"Take care of him, the best you can," I said, just as the dog scratched at the gleaming black paint of the driver's side door. I cringed. "I ain't expecting miracles."

I opened the car's door and slid inside.

"I apologize for not getting out," the driver said.

"No one does," I said.

The next week, the next trip, the dog wedged himself between me and the door, so I could not close it, and tried to clamber inside. When I finally pushed him back enough to shut it, he sat there looking up to the window, forlorn.

"Thank you for not running over my dog," I told the driver.

"He's a good-lookin' boy," the driver said.

"Looks ain't his problem," I said.

The dog tried to herd us back to the cabin, but the driver was patient, careful.

I rolled the window down to yell at the dog, but I didn't have the heart.

"I'll be right back," I told him as we pulled away.

It occurred to me that it seemed like the dog had been here for a year at least. His life was big, that way. In fact, he had churned up all this misery in just a few months.

"We have a dog," the driver said as we headed east toward Atlanta. "She's a sweetheart, a house dog. She's not . . . like that."

"He's what I got," I said.

EIGHT

In a Lake of Fire

OUR DADDY owned fighting dogs. They fought in a pit, sometimes to the death. Men drank bootleg whiskey and bet the light bill.

Sam had a pet dog, a big, beautiful boxer, in the fall of 1965. One day my daddy put a chain on it and led it to the car, thinking he might win some drinking money.

My brother was eight years old. He never had another pet, a dog just to love on. There is no point in dwelling on it. I am just saying there is a backstory to almost everything.

•

He went to work in a coal yard when he was nine, did pick-and-shovel work at eleven, loaded boxcars at the clay plant at fourteen. He spent most of his boyhood lying under a broke-down tractor, truck, or other junk, trying to cuss a rusted-on part to twist free. And every night, once the weather had turned and the snakes went into their holes, he followed his dogs through the briars and deadfalls, as if, even in the happiest times, life had to be wickedly hard. He was miserable sitting still, so what could be better than chasing a dog across a mountain, and the mountain beyond? But they were *not* pets, he is quick to tell you; they had a purpose, and worked for a living.

As a teenager, he had just enough money to feed his dogs, but none to baby them. They lived on a heavy chain fixed to an iron stob that was pounded three feet into the clay, or in pens woven from dog wire and tar paper and slat pine. They sheltered in doghouses hammered together with bent nails from scrap plywood and tar paper, insulated in cold weather with hay and pine straw and old quilts. As a boy I thought it was odd how there were never any sharp corners on the houses, till I saw my brother's possum and coon dogs, in boredom, gnawing their own house.

"I didn't have no money to do better by them," he told me, but they were the most valuable thing he owned, even more valuable than a faded-blue,

prewar Willys panel truck he turned into a jeep.
He was too young to drive, except on the rutted,
muddy mountain roads, where a tag or license was
unnecessary. He and his friends pushed it more
than he drove it, which was probably the safest
thing, though once he did get it going fast enough
to run into a tree and break a leg.

"You buy your groceries, pay your rent, your
light bill, and get enough gas to make it to work
that week so you can work enough to pay for it
all the next week, and there wadn't nothin' left
over, not for people and sure not for dogs," said
my brother, who, as he got older, made his living
in the nerve-shredding clatter of the town's cotton
mill. "I took care of my dogs the best I could."

They drank from five-gallon buckets scrounged
from construction sites, and ate from upside-
down, baby-moon hubcaps and ancient, burnt-up
biscuit pans. But the doghouses were wind- and
watertight. In hot weather they got fresh water
twice a day, and in freezing weather he went out
and broke the ice in the buckets with the hickory
handle from an old sledgehammer. He pulled the
ticks off them in summer, and dusted them for
fleas with big handfuls of flea and tick medicine
intended for cows. He dunked them in burnt motor
oil, to treat their mange.

As a child, I was fascinated by those dogs, by all dogs, I suppose. They were all muscle and hard heads, a mix of redbones, blueticks, and black and tans, not registered dogs, but they would by God hunt. They were, in a way, discarded dogs, too, used up and bad tempered, the kind of dog you sold to a boy for fifteen dollars or swapped him for a day's work cutting pulpwood. My brother told me not to, but I used to pet them when I was a boy. I felt sorry for them. The hounds looked like what I imagined old gladiators to be, crisscrossed with white scars. Some were missing an ear, or two, and were deaf as a stone, and others had their noses split open. Not one had a full set of teeth. Some were a little lame, and their once-beautiful voices had weakened, thinned.

My brother eked the last few hunts, the last few miles, out of them, like he did with that old jeep. He was neither gentle about it nor cruel. He knew what they lived for, so maybe there was a kindness in it, I suppose. He took dogs with a lifetime of bad habits, the biters and wanderers, and trained them to *behave,* taught useless dogs to hunt by pairing them with old dogs with the patience to tolerate a yapping amateur. Later in life he would have purebred dogs that were more machines than flesh and blood, but in those early days he had to kick them off a false tree, or kick them apart when they fought, to keep them from murdering one another out on the hunt.

"I ain't never been mean to a dog," he told me, and in the time and place that shaped him, I have no doubt he believed that to be true. "My dogs minded better than most people's kids."

They suffered in the summers. They seemed wasted and half alive on the chain in the months when the snakes were out, when walking the mountains was not just illegal, it was suicide. Then, as the weather cooled, they would hear the metallic clang of a tailgate and rise up out of the dirt, baying, twisting, and straining at the chain, till my brother freed them and they bolted to the truck. The dogs would pile in the jeep, dancing, quivering, snapping. A gaggle of boys, just as raggedy, would pile in among them, and together go bouncing up some fire road to a bleak, dark, random place, until the battery went dead or its bald tires lost their grip in the mud.

The dogs would tumble out and disappear into the black, till one of them picked up a scent and the music began. It remains one of the most beautiful sounds I have ever heard, like it was in the trees and not these scarred, chewed-on, desolate creatures. In it was a single message.

Hurry.

I don't remember ever seeing him pet one of his dogs or talk to them, except to command, but I guess that wasn't unusual. "I never petted my dogs unless they done good on the tree," he said. But he would walk all night to find a lost dog, refusing to trust that it would find its way home. He almost drowned one night to save a dog that was trapped in a deep creek under an overhang of roots. The dog was treading water, barking nonstop. It was below freezing that night, but Sam jumped in the bitter-cold water and lifted the dog over his head till he could figure a way out, then carried it for miles, his clothes freezing on his back. His dogs were never pampered, seldom even petted, but they died in the shade, of old age.

•

My dog did not work for a living. His herding had, so far, mostly been a loud, violent journey to nowhere. He had shown us, so far, no other, obvious purpose, "'less you count fightin', and stinkin'," my brother said. This was, I believed, mostly unfair. Speck was one of those outside dogs who did not greatly stink, unless he was covered in some fresh abomination, but I have to admit that his hygiene, in that first year, was embarrassing. Sam had a horror, a phobia, that the dog might slip into the house, and I did not tell him he already had; he usually curled up in Sam's chair.

"If it's got more than two legs," he said, "it stays outside."

"Absolutely," I said.

I had tried, every month or so, to bathe the dog, and made a pitiful attempt to groom him. He acted like I was killing him, bit me three times, and jumped out of the washtub before I got all four feet in. I guess you could say I washed him in installments, in pieces, but if you wash three-sixteenths of a dog, that still leaves a great expanse of dog unwashed. I even tried the choke chain, which he used to attempt suicide; he would rather die than be clean. I chased him around the place with a pair of scissors—and sometimes my pocketknife—trying to hack away knots of matted hair. Now and then I would get one, and hold it in triumph in my upraised fist, like a scalp.

The dog had a way with making a simple thing very hard. I kept his teeth in good shape with chew toys and bones, and I was religious about his shots and medicine and overall health, but had all but given up on the aesthetics. He forced my hand, finally, by rolling joyfully in the carcass of a deer.

He did not just roll in it, he wallowed, submerged. By fall, he smelled like things I cannot say. I can bear up to most things in this life, but I was not man enough to groom and bathe him myself. And the one person I could go to for help was the last one I wanted to ask.

●

He was not the kind of dog you usually gave a haircut, but we didn't know that then, and his tangled coat was in such miserable shape that I had to do something before I could bathe him. I could have taken him to a groomer, but when I called a professional she said she would have to keep him in a cage, maybe for hours, waiting his turn. I knew he would hate that, and I wasn't sure how he would respond to being handled. Some people have no sense of humor about being bit.

I gave it one more try. I got a grip on his collar with one hand and went to work with a pair of scissors, being careful not to get anywhere near his eyes. With him fighting me nonstop, I got out an accumulation of beggar lice, cow weed, blackberry twigs, and a surprising number of late-season bugs that had hitched a ride, but his coat was still matted beyond anything I had ever seen.

I went to the pet store, for tools. They were all apparently plated with platinum, and looked too flimsy for what I needed. Sam went with me, just to make disapproving sounds.

"Use the one you cut your hair with," he said, and I told him no.

I had cut my own hair, mostly, for forty years; it wasn't that I was unwilling to spend the money on a good barber, it was finding time to sit an hour in a waiting room. Besides, I didn't like the idea of a stranger touching me around the head only to find, when they were done, I still looked like me. I was not expecting a movie star, but I was not expecting just me, with bigger ears.

I told my brother I still had a sliver of pride left and would not cut my hair and my dog's hair with the same utensil. So, we went to Walmart. I found a good brush and sturdy clippers that did not require long-term financing. At home, I put the dog on a chain. He watched me, trusting, till I hit the ON button, and the buzzing, like a hive of bees trapped in a five-gallon bucket, commenced. The dog backed up and looked at me like I was holding a chainsaw, and tried to hang himself.

I walked into the house, beaten.

"I need help," I told my brother.

He had worked ten hours that day, cutting

acre after acre of ball fields and parks on a zero-turn mower for the city's Parks and Recreation Department, where he went to work after the cotton mill closed down. It was fall everywhere else in the world but here, where it was still summer, still miserable. He wearily pushed out of his chair and followed me outside.

●

For two hours, he gently helped me groom a scared dog. Sam had a way with frightened dogs and animals in general, a kind of calm, firm purpose. I held the chain and tried to hold the dog still as Sam ran the clippers over his matted mess of fur. I thought, once or twice, he was going to gag.

"You know how to do this?" I asked him.

"Oh, yeah," he said.

"You've done it before, then?"

"Nope," he said.

Hounds are shorthaired dogs. You don't groom hounds, much. They got their baths crossing streams and rivers. But to him, like me, it seemed like a simple thing, like mowing grass.

We cut two bushels of hair off the dog, at least. We believed we were doing a good job. We really did.

When we were done, he looked like a chicken

that had blown through a factory fan. He had gaps and gullies in his coat, and muttonchop whiskers where his once-handsome face used to be. We had missed some parts of him completely, and shaved parts of him almost to the bone. Foot-long wisps of uncut hair wafted in the breeze like tall weeds in a field of short grass. He was lumpy and bumpy and jagged and furrowed and—in some sad patches— damned near shiny.

"Looks good," I said.

"Yeah," he said, "looks good."

In our defense, the sun set halfway through our barbering, and our outside lights are pretty dim, so we did it partly by feel. The dog felt better, immediately. He had suffered under all that mess. He had been wild-eyed and panting through the ordeal, but forgave us as soon as we turned off the clippers and he sat between us on the driveway. He was, all of a sudden, unafraid of my brother. Sam petted him once, then twice. Speck waited patiently at his leg for more, but two was all Sam had in him, and he retreated into the house. The bath, I assumed, was my burden alone.

I have heard that it is a sign of insanity, to do the same thing over and over, expecting a different result. I don't know why I believed this time would be better.

I had filled a big tub with water to let it warm in

the sun and brought out an economy-sized bottle of Mane 'n Tail, which was good enough for my girl cousins and I figured it was good enough for him. I do not think I have words to describe how bad a thing this turned out to be. As always, he believed I was drowning him, and ran away half washed and twice half rinsed, and I had to crawl under my truck, three times, to drag him out and carry him to the bath. I hurt my back and further traumatized my dog. My brother came out and told me it would be easier, next time.

"I don't think I will live long enough," I said, when I was finally done, "to ever want to do this again."

I was sure he would go wallow in a mudhole once I was through, but instead he found some grease on the underside of the tractor or one of the trucks, and, somewhere on the mountain close by, one tiny dot of an unspecified manure. I think it was cat. One speck of cat manure smells worse than an entire decomposing cow. He smelled worse, looked worse, than before this began.

My brother said goodnight to our mom, then crawled wearily into his truck. It always surprises me when he looks a little stooped over. I often joke that he is getting old, but I never mean it; he is unchanging, indestructible, as strong as when he was a teenager. But he is almost sixty-four now, and a lifetime of hard manual labor is beginning to nick at him, and pull him closer to the ground.

But it was a good day. After all these years, we finally had something in common. Speck was the living proof. We were, my brother and me, the two sorriest dog groomers in the world.

"I appreciate it," I said to him as he slammed the door.

He just nodded.

"I know you don't think much of him," I said.

He shrugged and twisted the key, then rolled down his window as he inched down the driveway with his foot on the brake; it was his way of always having the last word.

"Just don't get too close to him," he said. "If you don't never get close to a dog, he'll be around forever."

NINE

Tumbling, Tumbling Down

A BOY should have had this dog, a tireless, terrible, indestructible boy. Every bang of the screen door would have been the start of a great race. Think of the mud puddles, alone. Think of the adventures. The days would flash by, time would catch fire.

•

I ran with all the grace and speed of a potbelly stove. Over the years I had broken both legs twice and ruined one knee, and there I was, running in slow motion and leaping, sometimes, whole inches off the ground.

The dog didn't care. The dog was thrilled. Finally, something to herd that did not try to kick his skull in. Every night, after supper, we played in the yard.

"That dog'll trip you," Sam warned.

"Nah," I said.

It must have looked pitiful, from a distance. But it made me, for at least a little while, less of a miserable, crabby old grouch. All I had to do was clap my hands or talk to him in that goofy, enthusiastic way that people do, and he was bouncing, the way dogs do. I'm not saying it was anything that has not happened on this planet a billion or so times before; I am only saying it made me laugh out loud, again, a little bit, and the dog woofed and growled and hunkered down and then leapt like that asphalt driveway was a trampoline.

"Who's a *gooooooooood boy?* Who's a good Speckle?"

He would whirl, around and around, answering the best he could.

I AM!

I AM!

I AM!

It made me think of one of my favorite dog books, *My Dog Skip,* by the great Mississippi writer Willie Morris. It was just a thin little book about a boy and his dog, but the thing that made it so good was that Willie, a lifetime later, had never lost the wonder of it. It had a boy's joy, and a dog's, too. *It had to do with that look in his eye when he was around baseball . . .*

It was worth all the trouble he caused, as his first summer here passed into his first fall, to see a living thing that happy. I would take off running in one direction, and he would cut me off in a flash, and try to herd me another way. I would rough him up, pulling at his fur and ears, and push him one way as I stumbled off in another. He was faster and more nimble, but I had two good eyes.

I would spin him around and come up on his blind side.

"Here I am," and he would whirl.

But I'd cross over to the blind side, again.

"No, wait. Here I am."

It was probably a little mean, but it was the only edge I had. But he had formed an idea in his head of where he wanted me to be, and he was going to push and nudge me there, cut me off when I tried to stray, and even nip at my heels, like he did the mule's, if I wasn't moving fast enough to suit him. It was kind of beautiful.

We played it till I was staggering and sucking wind, played longer than we should have. I did one of my lightning-quick, balletlike crossover moves from his blind side and he stepped right under me, right where the driveway began its steep slope to the pasture.

I fell.

The dog was not to blame. It was just gravity, and the slow accumulation of years.

It was either stomp and crush my dog or careen down the hill, and I went flailing like the fool I was. I almost made it, almost got my balance back and my feet under me, but the dog rushed up to help, and tripped me again. I landed hard on the asphalt on my left knee; I thought I actually heard the flesh burst open. But I just kept falling, like I was some kind of cartoon. I gouged three deep holes in my left palm. I rolled, with all the comical momentum of a big man out of control, and even managed to injure my tailbone and gash open the back of my stupid head.

I sat there, blood running down my leg, my knee ballooning and getting tight, and feeling like a moron. With my luck I had cracked the bone, or . . .

The dog whined.

It took several long seconds to realize, to really hear it. You couldn't hurt the dog enough to get a sound out of him, except maybe a growl or snarl, but he sat there beside me on the asphalt and whined. I guess there was no great clairvoyance or intuition in it, on his part, what with all that blood and all. It was still a surprise. I was the one who landed as brittle as a piano heaved from a window in a silent movie, but it was my dog who was crying.

I rubbed his head, and told him I was all right.

"We got to stop bleeding on the driveway, you and me," I said to him.

I didn't think I had broken anything, but if I had, it could wait.

"I think I'll just lie here a minute," I told the dog.

I have always resented gung-ho people who say, *When you get knocked down, pick yourself right back up.* I think a young person made that up. Sometimes—and I speak from great experience—it is better to stay down awhile, catch up on some rest, and think about life as you know it. The world will spin on just fine, for a while, and I could try to catch up later, if I was able. You would be surprised how soft the asphalt can feel.

I fell down my front steps once in New Orleans, at the corner of Joseph and Annunciation Streets. The details are not important, but I lay there a long, long time, till I remembered I was in New Orleans, and thought somebody might come by and try to harvest any organs that might still be viable.

This was a lot like that. *At least,* I thought to myself, *no one was looking.*

"What happened to you?"

My brother was standing over me. I hadn't heard him come up. Perhaps I had damaged an eardrum.

"Fell down," I said.

"The dog trip you?" he asked.

"Nope," I said.

"You need some help gettin' up?" he asked.

"Nope," I said.

"You gonna get up?"

"Nope."

"Probably ought to," he said.

"I'm just gonna sit here awhile," I said.

"Okay," he said, but he didn't leave.

"You break anything?"

"I don't know. I don't think so."

My mother and sister-in-law watched from the porch.

"Dog tripped him," he told them.

"He's not hurt bad, is he?" I heard my mother ask.

"Naw," my brother said.

"Is the dog hurt? He didn't fall *on* the dog?" she asked.

"Me and the dog are fine," I shouted to her. It made me a little mad, to be discussed like I was a plant, or a mailbox.

"Well, then, what's he doing?" she asked, continuing to ignore me.

"He's just sittin' out there bleedin' on the driveway with that stupid dog," my brother said, and they all just crowded onto the porch and watched me awhile, I guess to make sure I did not get up and fall down again, or just roll on down the hill into the pasture, or perhaps into the road.

"He don't get up in a minute or two, I'll drag him in," Sam told them, and they all went back inside, more or less satisfied, to discuss how some people in the family just needed Jesus. I struggled up not long after that and limped slowly to the house. I couldn't let my brother tote me in; he would have brought it up twice a month for the rest of my life.

The dog followed me to the door and lay down against it, till I limped out and assured him that I was not going to die. He waited by the door a long time, for snacks, probably, but it can't hurt to believe the best in a dog.

I tried to keep up as the first Christmas lights began to blink on across the brick ranchers, frame houses, and mobile homes along the two-lane roads that link this small place with the wider world. I limped and staggered after him, sometimes cursing, flinging empty threats, till I

gave up and found a seat on the steps, to wait.
Sooner or later, he would come loping back to sit
beside me there, and wait for me to rub him on
his head, pull on his ears, and tell the same old lie.
The days did not flash by, time did not catch fire.
But it would be wrong to say that they dragged,
or lingered.

•

One night, as I played with the terrible dog, I took
a breath in the cold air that didn't feel quite right
in my chest. It happened again as I closed my eyes
to go to sleep. *It'll go away,* I told myself. It always
had. There was a lot wrong with me, in mind and
body, but I still believed I was tough enough to
wallow through and do what I needed, and that,
one day, I would turn my attention to taking care
of myself. There was time for that. There would
always be time to set it right.

"If anything happens to me," I said to my
brother, deadly serious, "you take care of my dog."

"Don't you put that on me," he said.

Sometime after midnight, I woke up and
couldn't breathe. I don't mean I found it hard
to breathe; it seemed there was no air in me.
Somehow, my brain kept working. Our small-

town hospital, just minutes away, had closed; *I might have made it there,* I thought, feeling bitterly sorry for myself. I couldn't spare the time for an ambulance to make the forty-mile round trip to the closest medical center; it didn't take a smart man to do the math. I banged out the door, gasping, to drive myself, mostly to remove myself from the house, so my mother would not have to see it.

I almost tripped over my dog as I flung open the door. I don't know how he knew what was happening to me; I guess whatever sixth sense he had when things were bad must have been pinging, and he whined and tried to herd me across the yard, but as usual he didn't know where he wanted me to go. I shoved him away and crawled into the cab, and he put his paws on the edge of my seat. I had to shove him out of the way, again, to close the door.

"You can't go, buddy," I croaked.

I careened from side to side in the driveway, the dog running beside the driver's side window; I couldn't hold my breath for three minutes, let alone thirty, the time it would take to drive to the emergency room. I just didn't know what else to do.

As I roared through the country roads, it occurred to me that I could call 911 and have the ambulance meet me, and my heart sank as I realized I had left the damn phone behind. I had always hated that phone, and thought, bitterly, that the one time I needed it, really needed it, I had left it behind.

It was a cold night, but the warm air from the heater, blowing in my face, made it even harder to breathe. My head swimming, I rolled down the window and, in that cold air pouring on my face, I caught the tiniest squeak of a breath.

.

The head nurse told me I did the right thing and maybe saved my own life, but she was kind. I would learn that my heart and kidneys were in failure and my lungs had filled with fluid, in part because of general stupidity and a long-term dependence on destructive medicines that had gone unregulated for too long. One of my lungs would collapse around the scar tissue there, from recurring pneumonia. All of this, just a few years after I walked free and easy from the oncologist's office in downtown Birmingham, thinking I was ten feet tall and bulletproof, after all.

I was useless, for a while.

A hill became a hateful ordeal.

A flight of stairs did me in.

I got pneumonia, and sat with a blanket on my legs.

I had, I realized, early onset old-man disease. Everything wrong with me was my own fault, and I *still* felt sorry for myself.

I came home to find the dog having some kind of fit. He rolled, leapt, almost floated on the air.

"I told him you were coming home," my mother said.

She believes in things like that, that a thing can be greater, somehow, than nature should allow.

"He knows, *exactly*," she said.

I had heard all my life that a dog is a healing thing; they lope down the halls in hospitals and nursing homes, making people smile, though I have often wondered if there were antibiotics yet for the germs my dog could spread. But for three months or so, when about all I could do was sit on the steps, he kept me company, and kept me entertained. I don't want to make more of it than it was, but he sat with me for hours, till a cat passed by. Then he tore the whole world up for a little while, till he came loping back, proud of himself. Then he settled back on the porch, to wait.

Sometimes you put yourself in a place in your life when a dog is the best company you can have.

My brother sat beside us, sometimes, in the early evening. We watched the leaves blow across the brown grass, listened to the crows. We didn't talk much then, didn't talk at all, sometimes. I didn't have anything good to say.

I was down, and I guess I was waiting for something to happen to shake me out of it. Something always had. I can't really explain it any better than that.

"If something happens to you," my brother said one night, out of the blue, "that dog will grieve hisself to death."

He got up and went inside.

The dog looked at me with his bad eye.

Well, hell, I thought.

•

We walked the place, parts of it I had never seen. We walked the logging road, and eased down to the orchard so he could run rabbits that lived in the maze of dormant trees. I had always heard land was healthy if it had rabbits, and I have never seen more rabbits than here. He ran them till his tongue was hanging out, never caught a one, and the next day he did it all over again, as if he had forgotten overnight the futility. One day, meandering, we saw a big buck along the fence in the upper pasture, forty yards away. He was the color of dark sand, with antlers like a chandelier. Speck went into some kind of dementia, and the buck seemed to levitate, leaving the ground in a slow arc that was so graceful, so effortless, it should not have even been possible. He floated over four strands of wire, chest high on a man, and vanished into the woods. Speck did everything but pass out, and by the time he gathered his wits and tried to run it down there was just the waving grass. But he yowled and growled and sniffed the air for an hour, at the *idea*.

And so, with me stumbling in the rear, the dog plowed into his second year on our little mountain, though it seemed as if he had been here much longer than that. I guess you could call it a rescue, because he would have died on that ridge. But other rescues, I think, take longer to reveal.

TEN

Magic Dogs

THE SAD THING IS, a long time ago, I wished for this.

It was the summer before second grade. I was crew cut, sunburned, shirtless, and barefoot, staring through the window of a Ford truck. The dogs, side by side on the bench seat, stared right back. They were long-haired herding dogs, the prettiest dogs I had ever seen.

Sam was close by, listening to the grown men talk about the weather on the edge of a dried-up mud puddle. The old men could talk three hours about rain.

"What kind of dogs are them?" I asked my brother.

He shook his head. It was what he did, instead of admitting he did not know something. They belonged to our neighbor, a respected farmer and cattleman named Paul Williams.

"They ain't from here," Sam told me.

"Well, where are they from?" I asked.

He shook his head again.

"He sent off for 'em," he said, and made it sound mysterious.

"Do you think he'd mind if I petted one?" I asked.

He shook his head, curtly this time, like it was a stupid question.

"They ain't for pettin'," he said.

They had blue eyes, like people. You could *see* them thinking.

"He got 'em to watch his cows," he said.

"Uh-uh," I said.

He nodded, gravely.

Magic.

Magic dogs.

I'd do anything, I remember thinking, *to have a dog like that.*

•

Mr. Paul owned acres of farmland and beautiful mountain pasture just across a red dirt road from where we lived. He had been to college at Auburn to study the science of soil, grass, corn, and cows, but he worked in the mud beside his hired help, and valued the opinions of men who had never made it to high school. We used to play on the relics of iron-wheeled tractors and hay rakes that his ancestors had worked to death and left to be covered over in rust and blackberry thickets. He wore a pith helmet and overalls, and drove his pickups till they almost shook apart in the ruts, because a new truck was just showing off. My brother worked for him, baling hay, cleaning out barns and corncribs, and sometimes just riding on the tractor, soaking up wisdom.

"Give me a silver dollar one time," Sam said. "It was worth a good bit."

Mostly, I remember his dogs, not hounds and mutts like we had, but dogs with papers, with a bloodline you could trace back for generations. He had a big collie that once tried to eat my uncle John, and a wiry Airedale, which my mother called "that dog with that beard on it." But it was his herding dogs, the shepherds, that I loved. They were so valuable they rode inside the cab of his truck. People, even grown-ups, would stop what they were doing and stare as they rode by.

Mr. Paul would always get out to talk to my uncles, but the dogs stayed, until he whistled or called them. Then they scrambled out and sat on either side of him, glued to his legs.

I finally worked up the nerve to ask if I could play with them, despite what my brother said, and he just smiled and said, Why, sure, son. But they wouldn't move from his side until he told them it was okay. Then they would run and jump and play like regular dogs. They whirled around and around me as I ran down the road, herding me, though I was too young to know it then.

I ran alongside the truck to his pasture, to watch them work the cows. Mr. Paul used them to separate sick animals, so he could doctor the cows for pink eye or spray a cut or a scrape or give one a dose of medicine. The dogs worked in tandem, nipping at the cows' heels to get them moving, weaving safely out of the way when one of the animals tried to hook them. I don't ever remember him saying a thing to get them started; they just knew. Sometimes they would move the whole herd, as if they had some kind of great power over it. Now and then one or more of the big bulls would take a stand in the islands of lightning-blasted cedars and blackberry bushes and had to be driven out; the dogs plunged in, fearless, and rooted them out, the bulls bellowing, the dogs dancing around those wicked horns. I held my breath. It was the bravest thing I ever saw.

And fifty years later, I found one just like them starving in the trees.

"So he's the same thing, more or less?" I asked my brother.

"More," he said, "or less."

•

No one seems to be sure if they were border collies or Australian shepherds, but in my mind they were almost identical to my bad dog.

I read everything I could find on the Australian shepherd, border collies, and all herding dogs. I found his picture in books, and on a chart on the wall of the vet's office.

"So he *is* an Australian shepherd," I said.

"Well," said Dr. Clanton, trying to be kind, "that's probably as good a thing to call him as any."

I didn't mind that he was not registered by the American Kennel Club. He couldn't help it if his momma was not particular, or if his daddy was a traveling man.

He had Australian shepherd *in him*, for sure.

. . . one of the smartest of breeds . . . quick, thoughtful . . .

His history was painted all over him. The merle coat and copper spots across his white face marked him; his ancestors were bred for toughness,

intelligence, and loyalty. He had red and blue
heeler in him, but more bulk, ten pounds or so,
than most males in his breed. That made me think
he might have Great Pyrenees in him, but it was
probably just those buttered biscuits. The name,
itself, was a misnomer. His breed was developed
in America, by Basque sheepherders in the West.
Cattlemen adopted the dogs; they fought coyotes,
wolves, mountain lions, even bears. In more
modern times they were rescue dogs, and searched
for survivors of bombings and earthquakes in the
rubble of fallen buildings. Rich folks used them
to watch over their children, and they were so
smart, the dog experts believed, they could even
hoodwink their own people.

"What do you reckon happened to mine?" I
wondered.

"Too many licks to the head," my brother said.

*. . . will invent games, to keep himself
entertained . . .*

I was beginning to wonder, already, that there
was more to him than we first believed. One day,
I caught him watching my mother as she filled a
clean plastic gallon Purex jug with water, in the
event of a busted water line, or Armageddon, I

suppose. She set the jug in a corner on the kitchen floor, then took the lid off a warm plate on the stove and handed him a biscuit. The day there are no biscuits, *that* will be the end of the world. The dog ate it in two bites and considered the jug.

He growled.

The jug stood its ground.

Later that afternoon, I caught him dragging it around the yard. Of all the strange things he did, this was the strangest. He had to have pushed it across the floor, and through the screen door, and off the porch. But why?

"He can keep it," my mother said. "I don't want to drink nothin' out of a jug he's been chewin' on, do you?"

"Not on a bet," I said.

He lay in the yard for hours, gnawing, till it finally sprang a leak. I retrieved the lid before he could swallow it.

"Go to town," I said.

. . . with an irresistible impulse to herd . . .

He butted the now-empty jug with his head or batted it with his paws to get it started skittering or tumbling down the hill, then chased it, and when it slowed he nipped at it with his teeth or nudged it with his nose. It took me awhile to figure it out. He was just bored. He was practicing, and he herded the battered jug, rolling, skittering, tumbling, for miles.

I thought, in a way, it was kind of brilliant.

"That dog leaves a lot of trash in the yard," my brother said.

In a week the jug was so abused and perforated from being herded, nipped, and gnawed that it flattened out, and he could finally get a good grip on it with his teeth. It was no good for skittering and chasing anymore, so he took to grabbing it in his teeth and flinging it into the air. He tried to catch it—he really tried—but it just came down and bonked him on the head. He kept at it, though, for the joy of flinging it. I gave him a fresh one now and then, either a bleach or milk jug, but I dared not take the old one away; he would make the switch himself when it felt right to him. Now and then I would approach the dog as he was gnawing on his jug and say:

"Who's jug is that? Is that your jug?"

And he would bark, in happiness.

Yesssssssssss . . .

Then I would circle back and say:

"Is that *my* jug?"

Grrrrrrrrrrrrrrrr . . .

"I'm gonna take it."

GRRRRRRRRRRRRRRRR . . .

And then I would grab it and try to run, but it was impossible with seventy-six pounds swinging on it.

One evening my brother and I came home from supper at the Rocket Drive-In to see Speck running on the mountain with a decrepit milk jug, slaloming through the trees . . . till he lost his grip slightly on the jug and it slipped down and covered his one good eye. He turned headfirst into a pine tree and almost knocked himself out.

"Damn," Sam said.

I had taken, ironically, to calling him my magic dog.

But, as it turned out, my sarcasm was a little premature.

. . . will herd anything . . . even birds . . .

It started with the blackbirds.

They lit by the thousands, to fill the trees and cover the grass of the pasture in big, black, ragged patches. The dog watched from the hilltop, agitated, almost dancing.

I like to think he was plotting, considering. But it may be it was just in his bones.

He took off at a run, but oddly quiet for a change. I thought he was just going to chase them into the air, but he came at them at a slant, leaning in on his good eye, as if he was aiming to push them into a tighter circle. And for a few glorious seconds, he by God pulled it off. I was sitting on the porch, but a man rises to his feet, for a miracle.

The birds on the brown, dormant grass began to tighten, bunch together, hopping, and you could almost see an order to it. There was, for a blink in time, a clear curve of black feathers on the ground as he raced around in a smooth arc; then, as it had to do, it blew up all around him. The blackbirds exploded from the ground and trees in a single whorl, enveloping him, as he leapt, snapped, and . . . they were gone, moving as one undulating mass through the low, gray clouds.

I found myself hurrying down the hill, like a little boy, *cheering,* as the blackbirds vanished. He could not follow a single bird in the air, but he followed that black cloud of birds across the field, till they finally disappeared, heading for, as far as me and the dog could tell, Tennessee.

For another few seconds he was as alone and forlorn as any dog I have ever seen. But it was kind of beautiful, in a way. I guess you just had to be there.

•

Later that year, he showed us an even better trick.

It had to do, as all magic does, with cats.

The society of cats here on the farm always reminded me of the tribe in *Lord of the Flies,* increasingly out of control, and you never knew when they were going to rise up and take over the world.

I asked my mother, once, for their names. I knew Spew, but not the rest.

"I'm eighty-three," she said. "I can't name thirteen cats."

They were surly, imperious, and uninterested. Every day, when they were just lounging around being cats, Speck tried to wake them up, round them up, bunch them together, and impose his will on their direction. They spit and scratched and fled in thirteen directions, leaving him so frustrated he whirled in place, bawling. They crisscrossed one another, climbed trees, and vanished into farm machinery. In more than a year, he had not succeeded in getting one awful cat to travel in one single direction he wanted it to go. You would think, in a year of perseverance, that would have happened once or twice by accident.

"I can't tell you the secret, buddy," I said, on the

porch. "I don't know it. Cats do what cats want to do. People, and dogs, got nothing to do with it."

"At least," I said, looking for a ray of sunshine, "you don't eat their poo."

I rubbed his head.

"That," I said, "is your shining light."

He seemed fascinated by kittens. They were cats that had not yet gone bad. He would nudge them around with his nose, herding them by brute force till a momma cat intervened. It amazed me, to see this rough-and-tumble dog trying to play with something so fragile. But he never hurt one of them, not even by accident.

He was watching, one afternoon, as a momma moved her babies, one by one, from their hiding place under the back porch to a bed my mother made for them in a corner of the garage.

This seemed to fascinate him.

So, there is a way . . .

He did not try to emulate the mother cat, did not try to move the babies in his jaws.

He figured out something else.

The kittens were about a month old when they came out of their hiding place to play. Speck was, at the time, worrying a thick paper feed sack, gnawing on it and pushing it around the garage. The babies had become used to the dog. Unafraid, they blundered close—too close.

Speck, seeing his chance, began to push them around the garage floor with his nose, and straight into the wide mouth of the sturdy paper sack. I don't know if he did it on purpose. If he did, it was by God genius.

Then he took them for a ride.

He started pushing the sack around the yard with his nose, butting the bag with his head. My sister-in-law and mother were working in the flowers, and heard the kittens begin to cry:

Mew, mew, mew!

Hollering at him to stop, they hurried after him to save them. At this point Speck snatched the bag up in his teeth and ran. I don't know if he even understands the purpose of a sack, but as he ran he held the open end in his teeth so that they would not fall out, and took the kittens for a wild ride across the yard.

Mew, mew, mew!

My sister-in-law, Teresa, who loves cats, finally cut him off, and snatched the bag from him.

"But he wanted it back," she said, and he leapt, over and over again, to try to pull it out of her hands. She is not a tall person, and fled to the house while holding the bag of kittens high over her head.

In the garage, she and my mother gently extracted the kittens, who were by now dizzy and mightily confused. They staggered sideways across the concrete floor.

"Bad dog!" my sister-in-law said.

"Bad dog!" my mother said.

He bounced and rambled and rolled in the dirt.

And I thought about those fancy contestants in the Westminster dog show, how the commentators always said that the winners knew, absolutely, when they had won.

He knew.

. . . kind, loving . . .

If that was all he did, I guess it was enough. When he was thrown away, he lost the people he was assigned to protect, by his genetic code, and that explained, maybe, why he always seemed to be searching when he was on the road. And it explained why, when he found some kindness, he held on. He was my dog, of course, but when my mother walked to her garden or to feed her pets, he made every step, watching. He *knew* she was vulnerable.

"He's my dog sometimes," she said.

Now and then, to her horror, he crawled up on the foot of her bed as she tried to take her nap. It might as well have been a wildebeest, or a grizzly bear.

I guess that's just the way of all dogs, too. But he was part of something again, and in the most interesting way he became a kind of student of the land and its boundaries. Even my brother conceded that there was something special about the way he mapped the place in his mind.

He entered the main road just once, that I know of, to chase a pack of strays off the place, but otherwise would not get within thirty yards of it. But what was off was how he had figured out the other boundaries of our forty acres. The fence lines and dirt roads and driveways were easy markers, but he even seemed to know the lines that divided our trees from the timber company trees to the north and our neighbors to the west. It formed not a rectangle, as most tracts did, but a triangle; he knew it with eerie certainty, point to point, knew it the way the surveyor did when he drew it out, like he had left a paw print on the deed. He never stepped across those lines, that we saw. Even my obstinate brother was impressed. "I just don't get it," he said, "how he knows."

We had taken to just watching the dog, as if the mystery would suddenly reveal itself. As we sat, Speck peed on my truck tire, a shovel leaning on the garage wall, and the lawn mower.

"Yep," Sam said, "he's a genius."

We agreed on one thing, in the dog's second

year on our land. He had been a farm dog, surely, an outside dog. A house dog would not have squared off against the mule, or fought so viciously in the ditches, or, late at night, when his people were safe in their bed, preferred the company of the dark. He loved the gloom and the sounds, or maybe he just thought it was his duty.

But my mother said no.

"A child had this dog," she said.

Once, she believed, he had a gentle, pampered life. I walked into the living room one afternoon to find her in her chair and the dog on the floor in front of her. She appeared to be teaching him a game, a game people played with babies. Most call it peekaboo. We call it peep-eye.

She covered both her eyes with her palms, took them quickly away, and said, "Peeeeep-eye." The dog, lying on the floor in front of her, placed both paws over his eyes, then pulled them away. I wondered if I might be suffering an embolism, or if she was.

"That's right," she said. "Peeeeeeeeeep-eeeyeeee."

"How did you teach him that," I asked.

"I didn't," she said.

The dog covered his eyes again, then watched as she did the same.

The dog barked at her.

"Sorry," she said. "*Peeeeeeeeeep*-eeeeeyeeeeee."

The dog covered his eyes again, and the old woman laughed. It made him so happy he rolled over one whole rotation.

A child taught him, she said, or he was around someone with a baby.

"Somebody had to teach it to him," she said. "I mean, he wouldn't just *do* something like that, would he?"

"I don't know, Mom," I said. "They're supposed to be pretty smart."

She had taken, in his second year, to calling him "baby."

I asked her not to do that.

"Please don't," I said. "He's a man's dog."

"Okay," she said.

They played peep-eye for half an hour, till she decided he deserved a reward.

"Come on, baby," she said, and they went in the kitchen for a snack.

He is not a gentleman's dog, at least not anymore, not like the ones we saw when we were boys, and if he was a pampered pet, it was a long time ago.

But do you think a fancy dog ever herded a cat, or pushed a flock of birds across the sky, or played peep-eye with an old woman, to hear her laugh out loud? I understand that a dog, even a terrible dog, can be bred to be smart, but what a funny thing, that they can know how to be kind.

I told my brother about it, about the peep-eye, and how happy it made the codger.

He snorted. He actually made a snort.

"For a magic dog, he sure does shed a lot, sure does leave a lot of hair in the garage, and in the house, and blowin' across the yard. I can't kneel down out in the yard or lay down on the concrete to work on that ol' tractor without gettin' so much of that hair on me that I look like a Sasquatch, or a go-rilla. Bushels and bushels and BUSHELS of dog hair, pilin' up in the corners, just a-ridin' on the wind. I ain't never seen nothin' like it. I was outside, workin', and I saw a big ball of it, a ball of solid hair, just a-rollin' on by like a *tumbleweed* . . . you could make *mattresses* out of it, pillers . . ." I stood amazed. It was a salutation to dog hair, an ode to it, and I thought, as I walked off, that it would take a truly special dog to inspire a sonnet like that.

ELEVEN

When Dogs Will Fly

M OST DOGS live deep in the mystery of things. They fret and shake over weather a county away, and only their noses are smart. Skinny was different. Skinny lived in the light.

She was a half dozen breeds in one, combining to make something better than its parts should have naturally allowed. She did not dig in trash, or howl at phantoms in the woods. If you heard her voice, clear and bright, like a bell, she was hunting, singing to us.

The vet called her an excellent example of the Alabama brown dog, and she was the smartest dog I ever knew. She loved the family that took her in, too, and the hopeless Pup. But there was no place in her heart for Speck, just a kind of contempt. And the thing was, he was *trying*.

He had, almost inexorably, gotten gentler, better, had almost stopped stealing food and toys and picking fights and being an obnoxious lout. Well, okay, he still picked them, but he was getting better. There had been no serious battle for some time, in this, his second, year.

But I guess our dogs could hold a grudge.

He almost pleaded with them to let him play with them, dropping to his belly, like he was begging. But the Puppy saw this as an attack, and Skinny trotted away, nose, literally, in the air.

He would always find me, afterward. He would slide slowly, slowly down to the boards, like the air had just leaked out of him, and lie there with his chin on his paws.

Then, in what we believe to be her tenth year, Skinny became a different dog. She started meeting my truck at the top of the hill and, when I stepped out, would rear up and put her paws on my chest, blocking my way till I scratched her ears. Then she would go suddenly silly. She would hop across the driveway, one paw straight out, as if she were pointing, then turn and raise the other and hop the other way. I thought, at first, she suffered some kind of damage. Then, that quick, she would revert to her intelligent self. "But I caught you," I would tell her. "I caught you dancin'."

She would even sit on the other side of me when I was petting Speck, and demand equal time. It was like, overnight, she remembered how to enjoy being alive, the way Speck was, every day. Eventually they would bump into each other and snap and growl, but it was nice, in a way.

"Just a dog being a dog," my brother said.

It was in early winter of 2019 when I looked out the window and saw our dogs playing in the trees along the ridge, *all* of them, the Speckled Beauty, the Dancin' Skinny, and the Puppy McGraw.

I don't know why Skinny relented. I wish I had a telling, thoughtful story to tell. I don't know why the Puppy finally decided he was not going to be murdered in his bed, but there he went, running not for his life but just running, in what seemed a silly game of follow-the-leader. I just remember glancing out that kitchen window and seeing the world made straight for a little while.

I watched them scare up a squirrel, and there was something different about this squirrel from the million others they stumbled upon. I just know this was *the* squirrel, the one worthy of their attention. It raced up a scaly bark tree and Skinny put her paws on the trunk and began to sing. Pup bounced against the tree trunk over and over, like he was tied to it with a rubber band, as Speck appeared to suffer some kind of embolism. He joined Skinny in her serenade, though I doubt if he knew why, and his hoarse voice muddied her music the way a tone-deaf member of a good church choir can make a whole congregation cringe.

The next night, I heard a terrible brouhaha in the yard and ran out expecting to see them all tied up in a fight. Instead, I found all three staring, in bewilderment, at a possum that had keeled over in the backyard as if dead; then, as if they were all attached to the same live wire, I watched them jump three feet straight in the air when it came mysteriously to life. Skinny knew exactly what was happening, knew how a possum would sull to get a dog to leave it alone, then just kind of reanimate, but it was like she was playing along, for no other reason than the fun of it.

They chased the wild turkeys through the pasture, till they took off in that short, abbreviated flight. They flushed the quail out of the broom sage, and chased the jays and redbirds into the plum trees. They sent the big, black crows, as plump as chickens, shrieking to the barbed wire. Then they came running up the driveway, tongues out, content, as if they knew it was just a matter of time before the world finally righted itself, and dogs could fly.

•

It rained for four months that winter. I leaned on the shovel handle, cold water pouring down my neck and back and into the grave below. The red dirt ran loose under my boots and slate-colored clouds swallowed the tops of trees. It pressed down on us, made a box out of the world, and every day seemed like a mile underground. We lost Skinny, still waiting for a pretty day.

She died of an infection that spiraled into pneumonia. The nice people in the vet's office did all they could. The truce between our complicated dogs had lasted just a few months.

I remember thinking, as I carried her to my truck wrapped in a blanket, how it would be a shame to bury her in this running mud and gloom, and I even thought, sarcastically, if it would be too much to ask, for a good dog, for a day without rain.

Sam and I took a mattock and two shovels into a corner of the dormant orchard and hacked out a grave through the roots and privet bushes, next to where we had lain the lovely German shepherd we called Pretty Girl and a pygmy goat we never found time to name. There were prettier places here, but Sam said that here, in the tangle of bushes and thorns and vines, the grave would not be disturbed. Speck was not the only grave robber around. Besides, Skinny had loved the old orchard, and I guess there were worse places for a dog to lie than in a maze of privet bushes and plum thorns, where every day the fat rabbits thumped around over your bones.

When we were through, we just stood around awhile, unsure what to do then. The only real religion we had ever been around, either of us, was the Pentecostals, and they do not pray over dogs . . . or at least they are not supposed to. But I think the people who wrote that never met a dog like her. We stood there a long time in the rain, longer than we had stood over some people.

"Well," my brother said, "she was a good dog."

We slid the tools into the back of his truck. It was only then that I noticed the other two dogs, watching from the top of the hill, side by side. They would not come near, and milled around, restless. I expected Speck, at least, to come tumbling down the hill, to get in the way. But he never came close to the grave that day, and, as far as I know, he never has.

When we stepped from the truck Speck just wanted to be petted, and Puppy just wanted someone to run him down, pry loose his rubber ball, and throw it down a hill, fifty times.

"Seems wrong, that it would happen now," I said. "I mean, they were getting along."

My brother just nodded. For a man who could be gruff with living dogs, the death of one always left him with little to say.

•

The Puppy was a little lost after Skinny died. She was his compass. Now he lay in the yard, waiting, I believe, for Skinny to come floating up and lead him on some chase.

We always knew she was the one who did the thinking, but it was more than that. It was like her experience and smarts and excitement just seemed to crackle off her and light him up.

We made a fuss over him, and I threw the ball until I thought his heart would burst. When Speck stole it, as he inevitably did, I trudged over and pried it from his jaws, and gave it back.

He had been a pup forever, even with gray in his whiskers, and had fetched a million rubber balls in his strange and difficult way. He had a good life here, though he saw it from over his shoulder, always running away. He lost a fine friend when

Skinny died, but at least Speck, as flawed and unstable as he was, had mostly ceased chewing on his head.

He had people who cared for him despite his damage. It had taken him seven years to trust us enough not to run away or snap at our hands when we tried to pet him, and in another seven years, I think, he might have even let us pick him up. We thought he would be content in his corner of the big, scary world, but I guess he was more complicated than we knew.

I wish I could say that Speck worked some kind of magic and made it all better, that he became the Pup's best friend. But the little dog was afraid of him again, without Skinny.

Once in a while, you could see a trace of friendship, and they would run together in the woods like they had before she died, like the Pup just forgot, for a while.

There was one day when the mean ol' world seemed to wobble a bit. I heard a hissing and spitting and saw a big calico tomcat come streaking around the corner of the house, with a small dog on his tail, wild-eyed from joy or maybe fear but chasing it, just the same. And, a few steps behind, galloped Speck, gleeful, almost like he was egging him on.

It was the first brave thing I had ever seen the Pup do. It was bad, I guess, depending on your cat bias, but it was brave . . . till the tom had enough, turned on him, and he ran the other way.

●

One day, a pack of strays raced through the upper pasture, clustered around a girl dog in heat, and the Pup was swept up in that race. He had never shown any interest in a girl dog; I think it was just the pack itself, running. They vanished into the timber company land, a kind of wasteland of thick, seeded pines, choking briars, and creeping vines, and not much lived there but wood rats and snakes and stray dogs. It is what happens when you clear-cut the natural trees down to the red mud. Pup was not built for that life, had no meanness in him, and was too small to fight.

My mother said she saw Speck fly down to confront the dogs and fight them in the trees, till they turned and ran, taking the Pup with them. Speck followed, till they passed his invisible line, and then he just stopped and let them go. She said he tried to turn the Puppy back, but I think that is just the kind of thing an old woman wants to believe. We never saw the little dog again.

And suddenly there was just Speck. He did not mope around the yard, when he became the last dog on the place; he had seen so many strays come and go that I wondered if he marked them, marked their time with him, as other dogs do. I like to think he did, but I don't know.

He had, even as his torture of the Pup seemed to decline, always stolen at least one ball or toy to gnaw on. But after the little dog disappeared, he seemed to have no interest in them, and I never saw him with a ball again. The balls lay scattered around the yard for months. I would not pick them up, on the slim chance the Pup might one day wander back into the yard and grab them up inside that odd grimace. But there are thousands of trees here, and the leaves cover everything in time.

TWELVE

Dog Days

M Y PEOPLE do not go to psychiatrists, though they will hang a dead snake on a fence to make it rain, or pay a woman named Sadie five dollars to tell their fortune by gazing into the dregs of a coffee cup. We don't walk around telling people we are depressed, or that we suffer from anxiety. If a person gets down, they keep working, living. It's not real if you can't put a cast on it, or a built-up shoe, or a truss. No one, in the history of my family, has ever called their boss at the cotton mill or the steel plant to say, *Hey, Earl, I won't be in to work today. I'm working through some unresolved issues with my mother. Tell Homer to take over on the forklift.*

And if you do lay out of work, you better have a damn good reason, like a kidney stone, burst appendix, or a compound fracture, not because you are "conflicted" with, well, stuff. If you say you are at war with your inner child, you better be going into labor. We do not go to therapy. We do not talk about our feelings, unless it includes a quart of Wild Turkey, or a case of Pabst Blue Ribbon, and then we mostly just cry about our daddies.

We do not . . .

"Mr. Bragg," the receptionist said, "the doctor will see you now."

•

I hurried through the waiting room. It was the hardest part of coming here. It seemed like everyone was watching me even as I was watching them, trying to figure what kind of crazy they had. I tried to look normal, look very sane, like I wandered here by accident on my way to get a taco.

It was not my first time. I had been here two or three times before on the urging of other doctors, and people who cared about me. The clinical term, I believe, is that I just wasn't right.

The sleepless nights were the worst of it. That had worsened. Sometimes I could go almost a week with only an hour or so of sleep in a twenty-four-hour stretch, unless you count nodding off at traffic lights, or in the parking lot of the grocery, or at my desk, writing, my fingers on the keys.

And if I did sleep, even if only for a few minutes in a chair or the seat of my pickup, those minutes filled with terrible dreams. I thought, for a little while, I might really be going crazy. Everyone says that, *going crazy,* but it's not a cliché here; it runs in the family, but we just medicate ourselves with free cable and BC Powders, and keep walking, talking, till one day we do something too troubling to ignore or legally forgive, and the state takes us for a long ride in a white station wagon. And I wonder if my writing would be the same, if I do it with crayons.

But the nice doctor said, more or less, *pshaw.* He told me I was depressed, and that was nothing to be ashamed of, and what haunted me was a persistent anxiety, a less drastic medical condition, not a creeping case of the looney tunes. This was not, of course, his clinical language. And we talked about it, for as long as my good insurance and a one-hundred-dollar co-pay would allow.

I liked the doctor, but somehow it made me nervous, talking to him. I guess I was afraid that at any minute he would change his mind, get on his phone, and tell the white station wagon to pull around in front.

As I came in the door, the nice doctor asked me what was new.

So I told him about the dog
I *knew* the dog was crazy.

•

It was the season when all of nature seemed to go at least a little mad. I was coming back from the farmers' co-op in town, and I could see the heat wrinkle the air over the asphalt as I drove along the Mark Green Road. The trees, so green in midsummer they almost hurt your eyes, dulled to burnt brown and olive drab. The weeds in the pasture wilted, till it rained in the late afternoons and you could almost see them grow in the wet heat. The flies multiplied, along with the ticks, fire ants, yellow jackets, chiggers, and scorpions. If it stung or bit, it flourished, now.

As I neared the house I flushed two big crows off the carcass of an armadillo. Odd, how you never saw a live one, as if someone drove a truckload of them over from East Texas, and threw one out every twenty miles. I made my turn into the drive and hit the brakes, to let a king snake, shiny black and easily five feet long, cross in front of me. I watched it slither away, then I stared at the empty place where it used to be. Anything, to keep from stepping out into that slow burn.

It was months since I'd rushed to the hospital, months since I couldn't stagger up the hill to the doctor's office without stopping to rest. I had been doing better, just living in the slipstream of that rotten dog, when the days around me melted and the air clung to my face like cotton candy. I just kind of sipped at it, not wanting to risk anything more. It made me feel weak, useless.

I had been to get a load of horse feed, crushed corn for my brother's pigs, and a few bags of bricklayer's sand and mortar. The dusty eighty-pound sacks of mortar were heavier than they used to be. The heat sapped the strength and will right out of me, and by the time I even started unloading the lighter, fifty-pound feed sacks, I was about to fall down.

I usually enjoyed this kind of make-work. Even a simple thing, like clicking open a blade on a good pocketknife, was a kind of time machine for me; we used to work for hours, sharpening a broken-bladed, hand-me-down knife, testing it by shaving a patch of hair on one wrist.

But this was like walking in tar, and the

memories it brought to a boil were not porch swings and swimming holes and homemade peach ice cream. My mind drifted, wandered.

Where was that dog? He should have been here, underfoot . . .

I slit open the sacks and started to fill the bins. But the sorghum in the sweet feed was so strong in the hot air it took my breath away. I just kind of went slack in the white sunlight for a minute, and my head started to swim. There was still a sack left on the tailgate when I staggered into the shade, and into a broke-down chair. I would get my breath a minute, then get that last one.

Speck was immune, it seemed, to all of it. A long-haired dog, he should have suffered in that miserable heat, but if it even slowed him down it was impossible to tell. He would rush up, every hour or so, drink a gallon of fresh water, and lie for ten minutes in a cool patch of dirt he had wallowed out. Then he would dive back into the woods or into the waist-high grass of the pasture.

He picked fights with the timber wasps. An almost fluorescent orange in color, like nature painted them that way as a warning, and being stung by one was like being stabbed with a hot tenpenny nail. But they were easier for him to see, and he tried to bite them out of the air. He missed

more than he got, but there were consequences
either way. They stung his nose and lips and inside
his mouth, and it made me so mad—in a totally
unreasonable way—that I made it a mission
to wipe them out. I sprayed them almost into
extinction with Bengal Wasp & Hornet Killer, which
I think might contain plutonium, till they were a
ragged remnant of what they used to be.

As I sat, trying to get my breath, trying to swat
the flies away before they stuck to my wet skin, I
saw a solitary, belligerent timber wasp floating in
the heat. I'd get him, too, soon as I could move.

I had lived and worked in hot places all my life.
But this was the kind of heat you could smell in
your hair, like you were standing too close to a
seventy-five-watt bulb. And I wondered if this puny
feeling was all there was, from here on out.

*That stupid dog better not be in the rocks . . .
snakes in the rocks . . . snakes in the pond . . . snakes
in the road.*

The dying summer did not fade gently into
autumn here. It lurched to a mean end. I used to
track it, when I was a little boy, in a thin tube of
mercury on my grandma's kitchen wall.

94
95
96

I remembered, especially, a summer before I started school. I was in a garden burned up in the heat and eaten by stinging caterpillars, and I could feel the season through the soles of my bare feet. The air was thick and wet, but the ground was brittle; it was like walking on charcoal from a knocked-over grill.

97

98

My uncles would see me hopping from foot to foot on the burning ground and grin. They had seen this season come and go, and as stifling as it seemed there was nothing to it, much, just a slow turning of the earth. They would fish a wilted Camel out of their shirt pockets and wedge it in their dry lips, and wave a Zippo lighter across their face, a flame within a flame.

99

100

My grandma knew better. This was the season when nature turned against itself, when the land surrendered to fires underground. We would open our tomato sandwiches in the field or on a creek bank, and find scripture folded into wax paper. She was looking out for us the best she knew how. She warned us, every day, not to play with dogs. They were lethargic, unmoving, as they always were in the heat. But in Dog Days even a good boy would snap at you for no reason.

To a little boy, it was like something dreamed. Foxes staggered into the yards, rabid, biting at the air, and people shot them from the porch. Crows lined the fence, like undertakers. Our grandma warned us to watch where we stepped. The snakes were meaner, too. The coachwhip snakes would flog you to death, and black racers would form a hoop and roll after you down the road. None of that was true, of course, but it was gospel to people of a certain age.

But I have often wondered if the lore of it didn't save us from harm, somehow, by making us watch where we put our feet and hands. The bad snakes shed their skins in Dog Days, and left them, for a while, with a shroud covering on their eyes. They struck out blindly. Little, mean copperheads took shelter under porch steps, and moccasins slid into well houses and under washing machines. Deadly coral snakes, pretty bands of red, yellow, and black, no thicker than a pencil, curled in flowerpots. The newspapers ran photographs of diamondbacks that were longer than a man was tall.

101

102

The devil seemed close at hand. To fight him, the preachers erected white tents in fallow fields and abandoned parking lots, and led revivals late into the night. The people sat in metal folding chairs and beat the air with fans that had a blond-haired Jesus on one side and a funeral home advertisement on the other. My mother and aunts dragged us to the revivals so we could watch people getting saved, and hear "Old Rugged Cross" thumped out on electric guitar powered by a drop cord three miles long. The metal folding chairs were still hot to the touch, from being stacked on the bed of a flatbed truck in the heat of the day. I remember there was always an old, galvanized Igloo cooler on a folding table up near the altar, full of ice-cold water, and not one cup.

103

104

I went to sleep every night with my head on the windowsill, to catch the rare whisper of a breeze. It would ease any day now, my uncles said, as soon as the cotton opens, as soon as the first fat kid waddles by with a tuba round his middle on a Friday night, as soon as the first big, glowing Ferris wheel lights up the night at the county fair.

105 . . .

I was at the sawmill when it happened, when I smelled the sun catch my white-blond head afire

and lost my mind. I ran screaming, fighting, and
then my legs began to tremble and I passed out.
I came to a few minutes later, ashamed of myself,
as someone poured cold water from a Coke bottle
down the back of my neck. People said it was
sunstroke, an old-fashioned malady that has since
gone out of style, but my grandma knew better
than that. He was touched, she said. And it scared
me to death. Touched by who? But I was afraid
to ask.

A few days later, wandering barefoot near a
slough at the edge of the garden, I heard a rasping
in the grass at my feet. The water moccasin, as
thick as my wrist, was a gleaming brown-black; he
must have just shed his old skin. I tried to move,
but it was like one of those dreams you have, when
your limbs and lungs turn to wood. All I could do
was watch as it passed, so close to my dirty feet I
could have stooped over and picked it up.

•

I thought about it, often, this time of year. At least,
there in the shade, the butterflies that had fluttered
around in my chest had finally gone still.

I figured it was time to man up, lug in that last
bag of feed, and go find the stupid dog, and then
I heard that urgent bark, calling, begging. I don't

have my brother's gift, to follow a bark over miles, and against the ridge it seemed to bounce from place to place. Then I glimpsed a flash of white close to the pond, near the blackberry bushes that formed islands there. He was lunging at something on the ground, and I knew, with dread, what he had done. I ran to the shed and grabbed a shovel, threw it over the side gate into the pasture, and climbed over after it. I hurried down the hill, as fast as I could.

A cottonmouth, three feet long but as thick as my wrist at his fattest part, was coiled in a shallow ditch on the edge of the blackberries. The water snakes usually fled to the pond or the thick briars when they were threatened, but the stupid dog was between the snake and the water, and between the snake and the blackberry islands. It had nowhere to go except the open grass.

"Get BACK!" I yelled, but the dog was delirious. "GET . . . BACK!"

I grabbed for his collar with one hand and missed, trying to keep sight of the snake. No doubt what it was, not with the big, blunted triangle of a head, like the moving piece on a Ouija board, and the little neck and thick body and short, blunt tail. It was almost black under a veil of a dirty, rusty brown.

Speck was on his belly now, snarling, eye to eye with it, but I guess some old instinct kept him from lunging closer; I had seen dogs die from bites from smaller snakes. Moccasins are mean, almost belligerent—I don't care what they say on *Animal Planet*—and for a bad second or two I didn't have a clue what to do; I'd killed a hundred poisonous snakes, but not for a long time.

With the dog doing his best to get in the way, I stepped up and took one wild, off-balance jab, all the while trying to keep my boots far away, and cut deep into it about halfway down its body. Luck. It writhed crazily, and I stabbed down with the point, aiming at the head, and missed. The next jab, I almost cut the head away, and though it still writhed on the ground it was done. It was nothing to be proud of, and nothing that would keep me up late at night, either, just a snake that needed killing.

It writhed on for a good while, and I dragged the dog away; few things can hurt you twenty minutes after you cut off their head. Kicking him back, three or four more times, I cut the head cleanly away, scooped it up in the shovel blade, and threw it into the deep pond where the dog couldn't get at it.

I just stood for a minute, sweat pouring down

my face, leaning on the shovel handle. I meant to go hang the carcass on the barbed-wire fence, as per custom, but I was halfway up the hill with the disobedient dog and I wasn't about to double back. Later, I saw the crows hopping around the place where I killed it, and I knew that when I got there it would be gone.

My heart was still hammering in my chest, so strong I could feel it in my ears, and I was soaked in sweat from my hair to my shoes. But it was different now. It was just a heartbeat, not the end of the world, just sweat, just weather, just, as my uncles had assured me, the slow turning of the earth.

I heaved the last sack of feed over my shoulder and carried it into the shed to pour it up. As I turned to go inside, I looked at the big, swinging metal gate, ten feet long and five feet high. I tried to think of the last time I climbed over it, and it occurred to me I never had, till now. I am not saying I went over it like a squirrel monkey, but it made me happy, to have gotten over it at all.

I guess it's a little thing, an inconsequential thing, but it was the first time in a while I was not afraid of my next breath. The dog, still worked up, ran circles around the yard.

"I killed it, for God's sake," I said. "You didn't."

He rolled in the grass.

"Dumbass," I said.

He squirmed on his back, like he was swimming on dry land.

"Eat up in dumbass," I said.

The hum of the air conditioner reassured me there was a cool oasis on the other side of the cabin's door, but having survived the heat and the monsters of Dog Days I was a little reluctant to go inside. So I sat in the wet heat and talked to my dog, who took a full hour to wind down. Of all the kinds of crazy there may be, a man talking to his dog seems the most forgivable kind.

"Listen," I said, taking a grip on the fur around his neck, "you can't do that no more. We got lucky this time. If he'd of bit you, you might have died. And if one of them great big ones get you we won't even have time to get you to the doctor."

I told my brother about it that night. He just nodded, in that irritating way.

"I thought one of them big rattlers would have got him by now, as much as he likes to play up in them rocks," he said. They wouldn't bite, usually, if you left them alone, he said.

"So he ain't got a chance't," my brother said.

A week or later, the dog dug a harmless rat snake out of a gopher hole.

"Let . . . it . . . go!" I yelled, and he cocked his head to look at me, then kept digging. He clawed and bit till he had it out of its hole. It just wanted to get away.

At one point he had its tail in his mouth, and the look on his face, as I berated him, was so indignant that I had to stop and laugh.

I knew it was not a rattler from the pattern of its scales and the shape of its head, but unlike my big brother I have been wrong a time or two in my life.

"I hope it bites you," I said.

He barked at me.

"I ought to hold you and let it bite you," I said.

•

I didn't tell all that to the nice doctor, of course, just some of it.

The doctor was one of those quiet, careful talkers; he actually thought about what he was going to say before he engaged his mouth, a thing to which I was unaccustomed.

"I think the dog has been good for you," he said.

The dog, he said, gave me something to care about.

He was good company. He even filled up the corners where the worry lay.

People expect a lot, expect us to do right, and we fail them.

The dog, such a terrible, terrible dog, sat with me on the porch, just happy to be.

I think going to the doctor helped me, so of course I stopped after a while. I got busy with work, with contracts and deadlines and dangling participles. The medicine made it hard for me to write, so I quit it. But I would like to go back, someday, to tell the doctor a few more stories about my terrible dog, tell him he was right. Even if I never make it back, I like the idea that his value, as a dog, is recorded in the files of a Birmingham psychiatrist, where, as it turned out, I was not crazy after all.

THIRTEEN

The Return of Henry

THE FALL is a good time for dogs and fables. The broom sage turns yellow and the thick trees on the ridge are cloaked in color, and the snakes retreat deep into the ground. It seems like all the bedtime stories my mother told were set in this time of year, stories about deer, turkeys, raccoons, possums, rabbits, and untold gophers. The gophers wore bifocals, as I recall, and the possum had a vest and a cane. The dog loved the cool weather, and gamboled inside great whorls of blowing red and gold, chasing the characters of those old stories across the leaves. But they always came tiptoeing back, as if they knew all along the dog was just there to scare them, a little bit.

The real villain lurked in the deeper woods, but

he was coming, a cunning, almost mythical fox.
His name was Henry, but which Henry I cannot
say, since my mother named all the foxes Henry. It
has been that way since we got this place, about
sixteen years ago; we are, as near as I can tell, on
Henry VII, or Henry VIII.

"Every fox you hear is *not,* necessarily, Henry,"
I told the old woman.

"I know Henry when I hear him," she said.

"Well," I asked, "what do you want me to do?"

My mother, gentle soul that she was, wanted
me to shoot Henry, ventilate him, and tie his
stripedy tail to the radio antenna of my truck.
Once, I would have had no problem with it, but
things had changed since I got sick. I didn't have
much bloodlust anymore; it just leaked out of me,
somehow, after seeing so many people praying for
a little more life, a little more time.

Please don't misunderstand me. I am
hypocritical about it, arbitrary. I would shoot
a water moccasin or a rattlesnake without
compunction, the same way I would put my
bootheel to a black widow or a scorpion or a
brown recluse. I hunted much of my young
life, mostly quail, deer, and a pig or two, even
alligators, when I lived farther south; my hands are
as bloody as anyone's. But in a way I had already

begun to lose my yen for it, as the sport and the land itself changed.

I'm not saying I was ever any good at it, at the lore and the craft, but I learned it when there was an adventure in it, beside old men who hunted in overalls and ancient fedoras with century-old side-by-side shotguns loaded with slugs we called punkin' balls. They lured in big tom turkeys with homemade calls, trying, as one old hunter told me, "to sound like a dime store girl on a Friday night." I didn't know what that meant, but I never looked at a dime store quite the same.

Now, across my South, millionaires hunted big game in fences, where trophy animals eventually just ran into a corner to be penned in and shot down. They dressed up for dove shoots on plantations where they let the terrified birds out of wire cages, to be shot to pieces by rich guys who couldn't otherwise hit a bear in the ass with a handful of sand. It would have made my grandfather cry.

The wild is different; it is no longer wild, not like it was when I was a boy. Most of the predators are gone. So we marked our land with NO HUNTING signs, and my guns gathered dust on the wall, or vanished into a safe, though I guess they weren't worth much to anyone but me.

Once, on a fall day about ten years ago, I saw a tan bobcat in the woods along the ridge, almost invisible in the yellow leaves. And I knew, as I watched it pad silently away, I would probably never see another one.

Only the foxes, it seemed to me, lingered from the wilder times. Not much bigger than a beagle, they glided through the pasture and the woods, small and more muted in their color than the storybook red fox, all ears and tail, balanced on tiny feet, piercing the dark with a sharp, thin yip. A fox sounded like it looked, like something you would pet if it came close, but they were as smart—and as sly and vicious—as the storybooks made them out to be.

One fox, either the original Henry or his many reincarnations, haunted our land. He first appeared about fifteen years ago, and reappeared, year after bloody year. He did battle with the white German shepherd Pretty Girl, till bad hips finally crippled her, and then he matched wits with Skinny, who, we thought, had run Henry away for good. He destroyed, in one summer, eleven chickens, numerous biddies, fourteen ducks and ducklings, and an unspecified number of kittens.

It was just nature, but he was mean about it,

the old woman said. He left bloody feathers and grisly pieces of bone scattered around the yard. He would leave the vicinity when he had wiped out everything, till she got up the nerve again to get new pets, and the carnage began anew.

I have heard the old woman say only once or twice in her life that she hated something, but she hated Henry. In the foothills people attach all kind of magic and evil intent to wild things. But Henry's thin, high cry made her angry in a way I had seldom seen.

"Why did you name him Henry?" I asked her.

"'Cause I never have knowed a Henry I liked," she said.

My brothers waited years for a shot at him, but he was always too far, or moving too fast. He did not always wait till nighttime to do his mischief, and still he evaded us. My mother begged us to shoot him, but we failed her, and, night after night, she would hear him laughing at her.

"Cacklin', mean like," she said.

Sam said he thought Henry might be female, and the reason he/she was so voracious was that he/she had a den close by and was feeding pups. My mother ignored him, and exercised her right, as an octogenarian, to hear only what she wanted to hear.

•

One late afternoon that fall, I saw a big fox arcing through the pasture. It seemed to be almost playing.

My mother said she had heard him, late at night, told me he was coming to eat a litter of new kittens that had magically appeared, in that way kittens do, under the back porch.

"That's Henry," my mother said, when I pointed him out. With her eyes, it could have been a motor home or a riot of billy goats. "He will eat all my kittens." She said it so mournfully it left me little choice.

I went to the basement and came back with a lever-action Winchester, too much gun for a fox, but I had been tinkering with it and it was not locked away. I grabbed just two loose shells. I knew enough about foxes to know if I missed, there wouldn't be a second chance. I expected him to be long gone, but he was still in the pasture, about fifty yards away. The grass was full of field mice. I thought of moving closer, to a rest of some kind, against a tree or fence post, but I figured he would see me. I stopped at the top of the hill and snugged the walnut stock against my cheek. You don't forget how to shoot after a lifetime of it.

But he kept moving and I couldn't get a bead. So I waited, tracking him the best I could, looking at him beyond that tiny, blued-steel dot. The fox, like it sensed it, turned his head right at me.

"That's when you have to shoot," my brother had told me. "He'll look right at you, and that's the only chance you'll get."

I froze. I had forgotten to look for the dog. He had been running the mountain, on the other side of the house. It would be just like him, to run into a bullet.

I was still lost there, in between, when I heard:

AAAAAWWWWWWOOOOOOOOOOooooooooooooo oooo . . .

The fox evaporated. Speck, out of nowhere, blazed down the hill, chasing a ghost, and I pointed the rifle toward the ground and let the hammer down, easy. I racked the shells out onto the grass, cleaned them on my shirttail, put them in my pocket. I doubted I would ever need them again.

"You didn't shoot him," my mother said, when I came back in the house.

"Couldn't get a bead," I lied.

I wiped the Winchester off with a clean rag and put it away. I doubted I would need it again, either, but Southern men are funny about guns. They will pawn off the TV or wedding ring before they will part with a rifle. The only Southern men who got rid of an heirloom gun were falling-down drunks; a great thirst will pry it from them, but as soon as they sober up and get a little ahead they go back to the pawnshop, white-faced, shaking, to reclaim it.

This gun means something to me. One of these days, in slower times, I plan to hang it on the wall. It is an old Winchester Model 94 with a scarred walnut stock. Like most old guns, it has a story, too. It was a gift from my friend Mike; we rode motorcycles together, and hammered a transmission into an old MGB, before he went to the army. I played basketball with his brother, and his daddy coached our slow-pitch softball team. I gave the eulogy at his funeral, on a hill up the road from E.L. Green's store. We used to sit there and listen to old men lie, eating Lance's orange-colored peanut butter crackers and drinking Cokes with big chunks of ice frozen to them.

Look, I might of missed, anyway. But if I had pulled that trigger, and hit what I was shooting at, it would have erased one of the last wild things from this place, and smudged a good memory. The dog, just by being a dog, took that choice away. He did not have to be a magic dog, just a regular, clumsy, yapping kind. But that moral is lost on a lot of people.

I don't know what happened to Henry. My

mother never heard him again, cackling in the woods, so it may be he knows better than to mess with a dog like that. Sam does not believe in fables, much, but he agrees that the dog may keep Henry away forever. "The one good thing about that dog," he said, "is he runs *everything*."

•

I used to love those homemade stories when I was a boy. I went to sleep listening to them. I cannot remember a one, not all the way through. I only remember the feeling, like a hundred-year-old quilt floating down to cover me. I wonder if the dog will endure like that, if he will be a hero or a villain once all the telling is over. What if my know-it-all brother is the one left to say?

"I ain't never, NEVER, seen a sorrier dog," he said as the dog rushed up in the yard, not long after that, fresh from a roll in what was almost certainly mule manure. We watched him.

"Get away!" he said, and swatted at the dog with his hat.

"You'll hurt his feelings," I said.

"I have a weak stomach," he said.

The dog merely circled around behind him and sat at my side. He had learned, long ago, not to come up to my brother expecting a pet or a rub, even after the dog-grooming fiasco, even after Sam had finally stopped decorating him with Silver Creek tobacco, and gave him his haircut.

Some people just can't see the wonder in things. It reminded me of an old, one-eyed copy editor I once knew. We worked for the *Birmingham News* in a historic redbrick building downtown. He told me the newsroom once had an elegant washroom, with copper fixtures and tiled floors, the kind of place that made a poor reporter feel like a king. But the newspaper bosses tore it out, and replaced it with a leaky modern one that smelled like damp Sheetrock. "Because some people, son," he told me, "just can't 'preciate an elegant outhouse."

FOURTEEN

Of Mules and Men

I WATCHED SAM pet the giant mule's nose. She was calm, tranquil. He always had a kind of gift, that way. The secret, he told me, was to be slow and easy, but not timid. They could sense a timid man the same way they could sense a son of a bitch. A timid man, sooner or later, would become a jerky, twitchy man, and a farm animal, a horse, cow, dog, or even a great, black mule, just naturally despised a jerky man. As I leaned on the gate beside him, listening to the Gospel of Samuel, it occurred to me that it was the most words I had ever heard him say at one stretch, since his treatise on dog hair. The truth is that I like to hear my brother talk, and I have since we were boys. He talks out of the past, the way he learned it from people who taught everything else that was worth knowing.

"I'm not a jerky man," I said.

He said that was true.

"Well, if I'm not a jerky man, why doesn't she . . ."

He just kept rubbing her nose.

I gave up and walked to the house, mumbling.

"What's wrong now?" my mother asked.

"I'm pretty sure Sam just called me an S.O.B."

I used to think I was smarter than him, but not anymore. What he has is a wisdom. He knows what bait to use on a cloudy day, and how to ease a fish hook out of the finger of a screaming child. He knows if you wrap a blown fuse in a foil gum wrapper the car will crank and get you home, but if you leave it in, it will burn down to the engine block. He knows how to sharpen a chainsaw, lay block, and saddle break a Welsh pony. He knows which wrench will do, with a lot of slipping and blaspheming, and which is *just* right; you would be amazed how much eternal damnation lies between a one-half inch and a seven-sixteenth. He can string barbed wire, run a bulldozer and a pulpwood boom, and if you talk down to him he will fight you, as old as he is, because he just can't fathom living any other way, any more than he can understand sushi bars and spaceships.

If he had a philosophy, it would be that a man can't learn a damn thing without grinding a little

grease into his skin. You can only learn this world
if you wrap your hands around it and let it draw a
little blood. He just wants to live and work toward
a meager pension, decent health insurance, and
a paid-for house. He wants to eat a hamburger
steak once a week with Teresa and their daughter,
Meredith, on her day off at the Walmart, and
watch *The Virginian* with my mom with his supper
on a TV tray. He likes to ease around on Sundays
in his like-new Chevrolet; he plans to pay it off
about the same time he goes into a retirement he
still cannot fully comprehend.

By the time he was sixteen he was the single
strongest man I had ever known, not from lifting
weights but loading boxcars and logging trucks.
Even after he turned sixty-two he crawled under
houses with spiders falling down the neck of his
shirt and shinnied up trees with climbing spikes on
his legs; the only way you'd get me in the top of a
tree is if you dropped me there from a 707. He won
every fight we had, except one, when he got hung
up in barbed wire and I busted him with a rock.

Ten years ago, he and Teresa began to help
take care of Todd, her fifty-year-old brother who
has fragile X syndrome. He helps Sam around the
farm, though mostly he wanders off, uninterested,
mumbling about monkeys, till Sam, red-faced,

chases him down. He has tried to teach him to tie his shoes and tell time and count, but after ten years he still cannot tell his right from his left, and it is always 6:30. He has learned to count a little, though sometimes it is 1, 2, 3, 4, 5, 5, 5, 6, 8 . . . and then it's on to monkeys again. He sits beside Sam in his pickup, talking a stream of never-ending nonsense to the least nonsensical man I know, and while my brother grumbles and growls he is good to him. It would be unmanly not to be.

I came home because I was on the run, again, and stayed because of a sense of duty. He comes here every night and every weekend because he loves it here, loves the woods, pasture, pond, and all the hard work it takes to manage it. Here in this wide-open space, from the seat of a tractor or leaning on a pasture gate, things make sense. He is serenaded by katydids and crickets, swarmed by green flies, wasps, hornets, and worse, but it is a kind of paradise for him, I believe. He has bounced over every inch of it on that hateful tractor, the closest he could come to crossing it on muleback.

So, of course he and the mule would understand each other.

The mule was *created* to work, and so was he.

"This is a smart girl," he said, as he hand-fed the gigantic jackass a fistful of grass.

"'Cause she kicks a gate when she gets hungry?" I asked.

"'Cause she kicks it when she's *not*," my brother said.

I told him he might be right, again, but it was hard to like an animal that could, at any second, snuff out the life of your dog. He just shook his head, and opened the mule's upper lip, to check out her teeth. She would have bitten my fingers off if I did that.

"I don't think she'll hurt him now," he said, without turning around.

The mule looked at him with those big liquid eyes.

"If she really wanted to kill him," he said, "he'd already be dead."

He had noticed the change before I did. The dog still pilfered Bella's food, but now, at least most of the time, she just let it happen. She did not punt him into the wire anymore. They had improved from enmity to tolerance to, well, *pals,* in a few months, and ate supper together out of her trough. Some days he just lay there on the ground, nose resting on the trough, as she munched on her sweet feed. Now and then she nudged him back with her nose, playing with him.

He still raced down into the pasture to harangue

her and the other jackasses, to try to instigate a
stampede so he could try to herd them, which was
like hitting someone with your car so you could
practice first aid. But the frenzy of it, the kicking
and screaming, had slowly faded, and it ended,
usually, with the dog and his jackasses just loping
across the grass.

One evening I came out to feed them and saw
the mule standing in the grass, the dog sitting in
front of her, just looking at each other as if they
were having some kind of telepathic conversation.
The chemo patients warned me that, beyond the
confusion it could sometimes bring, it might also
create mild hallucinations. I guess that would
include dogs and mules having a chat.

I see them there, sometimes, nose to nose,
and think I ought to yell at him, in case she is
plotting his murder, still, but I just settle back into
my chair and let the evening wear down. I guess
my brother is right. What a fine animal, after all,
to be so tolerant of a terrible, aggravating dog.
And so, shamed and corrected, I ate my own
words about the mule, though I still don't step
behind her.

Sam said it was not one thing or the other that
brought this peace, but a convergence of things,
though not in so many words. Speck was still

an incorrigible, irredeemable, car-chasing, cat-wrangling, donkey-shit-diving, carcass-dragging, FedEx-blocking, bacon-hogging nimrod, but there had been a slow change in him; he was less crazed. Sam said he was merely older; he might finally be getting some modicum of sense, or else he was just getting tired.

The mule knew it, he said, because she was a watcher. She was better than a dog that way. She was smart enough to sense it, reason it out, he said. She had always had patience, at least patience enough not to kill him, though the dog pushed her to the bitter limit.

"I swear," he said, "I never would of thought he would of made it this far."

Now she actually seemed amused, even entertained.

"It just takes animals time to get used to each other," Sam said. "You got to let 'em work it out, let 'em figure out that they're not trying to hurt one another . . . he never did want to hurt her none; he just wanted to aggr'vate her to death. But it's never good to aggr'vate something that big. That dog, he lives to aggr'vate. If he couldn't aggr'vate somebody, why he'd roll over and die."

•

We walked down to the pasture to clean some weeds out of the creek that fed the pond, and the dog discovered a school of tiny bream, barely more than minnows, in the clear water.

He, for reasons known only to him, stuck his head under the water, for a better look. And, it being him, he tried to take a bite.

He came up sputtering, and coughing, and my brother, kneeling on the ground, just started to laugh. He never laughed at the dog, just shook his head in a kind of disappointment.

It got dark on us there, with the dog deep-sea diving into the water, again and again, learning nothing every time, except that every time it made us laugh out loud. Sam had settled down on one knee, and when he tried to rise to his feet he didn't have the strength. He reached out for my hand so I could pull him to his feet, and though it was a little thing it scared me half to death.

•

The doctors found a tumor in his pancreas. When Teresa told me, on the porch, I did not get tears in my eyes. I got burning mad, and went out behind the house and swung my fists at the empty air like a child. Then I sat for a long time in the seat of my truck in the yard, the dog sitting by the driver's side door, waiting, confused.

My brother could not have cancer, not this awful kind. Why, you might as well take that diagnosis and paint it on a granite statue in the old cemetery, for all the sense it made.

At first, as was his nature, he just shrugged it off. The doctors told him the cancer was treatable, and he would first undergo months of chemotherapy to shrink the tumor and ease it away from a crucial blood vessel—hopefully—before surgery to remove it. At first, before the chemo started, he didn't even mention it, and talked instead about hard-to-find tractor parts, and a clogged-up slough by the pond, and the plague of privet bushes in the pasture. He talked about which member of the city parks and rec crew was goofing off in the shade, and how we ought to go over to the fish hatchery in Centre, Alabama, and get some bass and bream to restock the pond. We talked, for days, about being boys, and the house we grew up in, and our grandma, and dogs.

The same cancer surgeon who operated on me seven years before would perform the operation at the University of Alabama in Birmingham, but mine was nothing compared to his. His surgery would take seven or eight hours, and even if

everything went just, just right he would be in
the hospital for a week or so and take months to
recover . . . if everything went just right.

First, he had to endure the chemo. Some people
glide through, some people slog, and some truly
suffer. It's odd, that it doesn't matter, sometimes,
how strong you are. It wrecked him.

I stood by and watched him dwindle, and
suddenly all the pains and complaints and
nonsense I believed to be so important meant not a
damn thing, just made me kind of ashamed.

•

It was hard sometimes to remember what the
point of it all was, all the work and worry and
things won and lost, as my brother wasted
away. It was like those times when you walk into
a big store and you can't recall what you came
for, but you just keep walking, hoping you will
remember.

One night, waiting for my brother and sister-
in-law to come by to eat, I fed the livestock and
settled into a chair to wait. I had come to dread
seeing him stumble weakly from the truck.

It is funny how a place, so lovely and green
and peaceful one day, can be empty, forlorn. I do

remember there had been no strays, certainly no pack of them, for several weeks on the road or in the woods. It happens sometimes, and you begin to think you might never see another wretched dog running in the ditches or ragweed again, that every dog in the world has a place to be.

The dog was missing again. He had disappeared into the trees at the far end of the place, as was his prerogative, chasing God knows what. He stayed gone, sometimes, for hours.

The pack of strays would have never gotten so close, otherwise. They materialized about dusk in the wild upper pasture, in the waist-high brambles, tangled, blackberry islands and dying Johnsongrass, so sharp it could cut you like a razor if you slid it through your hands.

There were four or five of them—it was hard to tell in the tall grass and weeds—and I watched them move into the lower pasture where the old woman kept her pets.

The little donkeys and misunderstood mule were far from the house, a half mile or more, almost to the main road. The dogs drifted closer, more curious, it seemed to me, than threatening. I had seen strays worry the little donkeys before, but we had Skinny then, who put them on the road.

My mother heard the donkeys begin to whinny

in that curious way, like it was the end of the world, and she came outside. She asked me to call them in, and I yelled as loud as I could:

"Bella! Buck! Mim! TIME TO EAT!" It was the only way you could expect a reaction out of a jackass, and they started to move toward the house and the side gate. The big mule and male donkey, Buck, trotted quickly up the hill, but in their haste they left little Mimi far behind. Mimi had a sore front hoof, a reoccurring problem that the vet had to address every year or two.

This was the last thing I wanted. I watched the dogs cross through the barbed wire and move in behind her. I don't think they meant to try to drag her down. But I was afraid they might scare her, and she might hurt herself. I know what people said about hungry strays, about what they did to small calves and other livestock, but I always mostly discounted it. They were just dogs.

Regular-sized donkeys are fierce, when it comes to wild dogs and coyotes, and will fight them rump to rump. The miniature donkeys had plenty of fight in them, too, but were just so small. The big mule was a murderous protector; it was why I seldom worried about them. But as Mimi hobbled up the hill, the dogs strung out behind, I decided to go down the hill and run them off.

I heard him before I saw him, crashing through the brush on the ridge.

Speck, believing that he was being called to dinner with everyone else, cleared the ridge like he was on rockets, and saw the dogs in the main pasture below him.

He had been waiting for this all his life.

He did what he was born to do.

He protected the herd.

He barreled down the hill and flew into them, and for a second I thought they would close on him and tear him up. But how do you take a bite out of thin air? He was spinning, snarling, ferocious, but in seconds there was no one to fight. The strays, all of them, just evaporated.

I expected Speck, as was his nature, to chase the pack into the trees and try to kill himself, again, but instead he got behind Mimi and pushed her up the hill toward the others, like he had suddenly, miraculously, found some sense. As soon as they were bunched together he ran a ragged circle around them, once, twice, then nudged them up the hill toward the cabin and side gate.

He was almost prancing, head high, sniffing the air. The excitement continued well into dark, the dog barking, running forays into the trees to make sure the strays had left, the mule and donkeys whinnying.

I figured it was safe to call in the dog.

"SPECK!

"HERE!"

He obeyed.

I'll be damn.

I heard him coming down from the hill, half sliding through the leaves. He almost knocked me down, and I grabbed him and would have lifted him off the ground, a thousand biscuits ago.

His breathing was labored, terrible.

It was one of those moments when I knew, utterly, what he wanted me to understand.

Did you see?

Did you see?

"I saw you, buddy," I said, and got a double handful of his fur and pulled him back and forth, side to side, roughing him up. He had that neon in his good eye, and then he tore off back down into the pasture, to see if anything down there wanted to be herded just the slightest bit more. But the ungrateful jackasses would not cooperate, so he raced back up the hill, demanding his reward. He had to settle for a peanut butter sandwich, and then he had to settle for another one.

He was a big hero, and that is the problem

with throwaway dogs. I wondered, as he pranced around the yard, if there was another Speck among those strays, just trying to get home.

●

I told Sam about it, and I admit I might have made it sound a little more heroic, considering the audience. His clothes hung on him, and he walked like he was not sure, in midstep, where he had intended to go. He did not say a word, just steadied himself on the back of a cheap plastic chair and eased himself down. He weighed around 230 pounds when he got sick, but was down to 150 now, for a man six feet tall. The dog ambled up and sat down next to him and I waited for the inevitable curse or swat, but my brother just laid his hand on his head and left it, rubbing between his ears with one finger.

I guess he thought the dog had finally done something worthy of it, or maybe his mind just wandered for a little while, or he forgot which dog he was petting.

"I ain't got no dog," he said, suddenly.

"I know, buddy," I said.

His last hound had died the year before, of old age.

"I'll rent you mine," I said.

"How much?" he asked.

"Fifteen dollars," I said.

"A week?" he asked.

"A day."

He never smiled.

"Naw," he said.

•

He was scared, for his own life, for the first time. He could not understand why he was just going away, pound by pound, a little more every day. He asked me, sometimes, why it was happening.

I always told him what I knew, and he always just nodded his head, like he understood, and then the next night he would ask me the same question.

We sat, every night, in those two chairs outside the shed where we kept the tractor. We ate supper, though he could keep almost nothing down, then went out and watched the dark.

The dog sat beside him, like he had figured out which one of us needed him more. When I got up, to get a drink or just step inside, he stayed there, instead of following me to the screen door like he usually did. Sam would say something a little nasty, sometimes, about his aroma, or the trash he dragged into the yard, but it always ended, somehow, with his hand on the dog's head.

You can say it was just a dog being a dog. Maybe that was all it had to be.

The surgery was scheduled in the spring of 2020, then the whole world got sick. As the coronavirus of 2020 filled the intensive care units in hospitals around the globe, the cancer doctors postponed his surgery. It would have made me crazy. He swallowed it with the other poisons, till the chemo was done and there was nothing to do now but wait.

They finally went ahead with the surgery, months later. Because of the virus, I couldn't come in the hospital with them and wait. So I waited in the truck, for eight hours.

Teresa called me in the afternoon. The surgeon got all the tumor, though there were lingering cells in the lymph nodes they would have to watch. We would have to wait and see. It seemed like that was always the diagnosis with this awful thing.

His mind, memory, were still fuzzy. He told the same little stories over and over.

"Just think about it," I said. "Now you're still right all the time, but you can't remember what you're right about."

I told him he even petted my dog.

He shook his head.

"That just don't sound like something I'd do."

•

Sam was in the backyard, piddling around in that slow, old man's gait, when he saw a flash of gray in the trees. It could have been a coyote, or a fox.

"Speck, heeeeeaaahhhh!" he sang out.

Speck sprang to his side like a show dog.

"Git 'im!"

The dog couldn't see what Sam saw, but he saw him point.

And he took off, almost blazing, till he found a scent, or a sound, and he was gone.

"You been training my dog?" I asked my brother, later.

He deigned not to answer.

Then, a little while later:

"He's a little bit of a show-off," he said, "ain't he?"

Speck was back in a matter of minutes. He ran up, dancing.

"Did you find a booger?" Sam asked him.

I think the dog was expecting a treat.

All he got was another pat on his head.

"Yeah," I said to him, "I'm looking better now, huh."

My brother saw a coyote inside a storage shed in town. It was in pretty sorry shape, gaunt and exhausted from running for its life from a whole world of people who believed it did not deserve to live, not here, not anywhere. It must have wandered in there to hide.

He looked at it a minute and then chased it outside. Once, he would have penned it there and shot it, but it was almost gone already. It ran into the woods and disappeared.

"If they're in town," he said, "then they're for sure out here."

If they were, they were invisible, but that was their trick.

One night, Speck and I were sitting in the yard and we heard that sound, like you took all the sadness of every stray dog in the world and distilled it into this. It would have been different, I guess, if it was close, but from the other side of a mountain they just seemed to be reminding us that, despite everything, they were still here.

Maybe they didn't belong here, but they seemed to fit, somehow, in the haunted hollers and high ridges, as if they moved into the empty space left by the original, wilder things.

Speck, standing against my knee, had turned to stone.

I instinctively took hold of his collar to keep him from running off, but there was no need. For the first time I could remember he stayed, just stayed, till that terrible sadness just blew away. When I went inside that night I tried to take him inside, thinking he might still run off and get himself killed, but he only turned and trotted off to his place in the trees, close enough to hear the mule and donkeys blow peacefully on the other side of the wire. He had work to do.

I wondered aloud, to my brother, if he thought my dog was spooked. He chuckled.

"They won't come anywhere near this place," he said, and put his hand on Speck's head. "You've got a real dog."

"You sure are being nice to him," I said.

He shook his head.

"We just figgered somethin' he's good for."

•

I guess we decided, all of us, to just by God keep walking. We graded off a place on the land for Meredith, his daughter, and finally cleared the privet bushes from the little creek that fed the pond, thinking it would make the ecology a little better when we restocked it with fish later this year. We spread a layer of river gravel and paving stones around the house, to make it a little easier for the old woman to walk. We planned to bring in some cows, some small Herefords, and maybe some goats, to help with the weeds.

We cleared the upper pasture, burning the brush in big, roaring, popping piles. I used to do it for two dollars an hour. Now I did it to make sure my once-indestructible brother did not stumble into the fire.

The dog would not come near the fire. He sat about fifty yards away, watching, till we staggered back up in the yard, covered in smut and ashes. The ash and smut made him sneeze uproariously, and for some reason this started him rolling across the drive, covering his nose with his paws, like he was a human.

We sank down in the chairs in front of the garage, to watch.

After a few minutes my brother just grunted.

"He's a show, ain't he?" he said.

"Yeah," I said.

We watched until full dark, just watched a dog being a dog.

"If something happens to me, you really do

have to take care of my dog," I told him. "Not just anybody can take care of him, you know that."

I waited a good while for an answer, but I expected to.

The lightning bugs were out. I have heard that there is a time of year when, instead of blinking on and off individually, they blink on and off as one. I have never seen it, not that I can recall, but I would like to.

The dog was jumping, snapping at the lights that came too close to him, like this was the first time he had ever seen them. He never caught one.

"All right," my brother said.

•

His first MRI in the fall showed that the disease had returned.

It always made me angry, before, when I heard people say that someone was fighting cancer, like it was something they could put their hands on, and choke the life out of. If you could do that, then my brother would break it to pieces in his hands, and live forever.

But it never drew a whimper from him. It was just always there, like a shadow you could barely see. But as I watched him work and live, month after month, to spite it, I finally understood what people meant.

He walked into the clinic in the fall of 2020, for another awful round of chemo, to live a little longer, to fight it by God a little longer. He suffered in ways I don't have the heart to say.

•

"The thing I hate," he said one day, with the terrible dog leaning on his knee, "is that I ain't got no legacy. I mean, you've got the books, when you die."

He had never said anything like this in our lives.

"Well, who do you think I write about?" I asked. "I've written all my life about the man you are. You've got a family, and friends, and more people in this town know you more than me. And not one of them has a bad word to say. They're lining up to say the same damn thing, that Sam Bragg is a good man . . . and I've heard a woman or two say you used to be good-looking, once."

We were sitting side by side, a few feet apart, but I didn't look at him and he didn't look at me.

It was the only way it could get said.

"You're the guy they depend on when things go bad, when they need somebody to pull them out of the ditch, or clear the road with your chainsaw, or jump them off in the middle of the night.

"People will line up to say this stuff over you, like they did Grandpa," I said. My kin could recall how they could see the headlights coming for miles down those twisting mountain roads, the night he left this earth. Sam was just three, but he swears he remembers it.

"People will remember you," I said, "remember what you did and what you said. They'll remember the truck you drove, and the fish you caught and the ball you played . . . and they'll remember you took care of your momma and your baby brothers in a cold house with no food on the table . . . ," and when we finally fled that life, down a railroad track in the dark, he walked in front, because even though he was seven years old he was already more grown than most people ever got, but somehow I couldn't get that part said.

"Well," he said, "ain't that ever'body?"

"No," I said. "Not by a damn sight."

"Those Southern men are gone," I said. "All that's left are a bunch of shiftless no-accounts who can't change a tire. You're the last real man. If I ever write a book on you, that's what I'll call it."

He studied on that a moment. I don't know if it

made him feel better or worse, but it needed to be said, and it was true.

He sat quietly awhile. The subject needed changing.

He pointed at the terrible dog.

"If he was mine, I'd turn him into a dog a man could be proud of," he said.

It made me think of a book title I had always loved: *World Enough and Time.*

"I think if we all lived to be a hundred, we wouldn't have time to get it done," I said, and he sighed, and said he reckoned so.

FIFTEEN

Quarantine

I N THE MORNINGS, after the dog's breakfast on the porch, the old woman lets him in the house to ambush me. I cannot say it surprises me, really. I hear him scratch at the basement door till she opens it, hear him dive down the steps . . .

Thump.

Clomp.

. . . like a box full of encyclopedias is tumbling down the stairs. He is the least sneaky dog in creation. How did he ever run down enough rodents, in his old life, to stay alive?

I hear him gathering speed the last few steps, hear the inevitable loud *thunk* as he slams sideways into the wall at the foot of the stairs, every single time, followed by the rapid *tick, tick, tick* of scrabbling toenails as he tries to get traction on the cement floor. He tries, and fails again, to make the sharp turn at my desk, slides to his belly, rights himself, and launches himself at the bed.

Ooooomph, I say, even though I have steeled myself for it, as he lands on my stomach or chest like a sack of fertilizer heaved from the loft of a barn.

Aaaack, I say as he sticks his face into mine, I guess to make sure, even after all this time, that it is still me.

"Get DOWN!"

I give up and kick and shove him to the foot of the bed, where he curls up for a nap. I am wide awake now, pretty sure it was his plan all along. I groan. I don't remember groaning before.

"He wanted to come down," the old woman shouts from the stairs, and I wonder when the wishes of this terrible dog began to override everything in our lives.

I know I should just heave him off the bed and run him outside, but I just don't have the heart. I go to work, which is exactly eleven steps away from where I go to sleep. I write, or try to, as the dog huffs and snorts, usually with his head resting on the ragged sweatshirt he snatched up on his way down. I was running low on towels, down to just three, and I had to give him something.

After a while, around lunchtime, I push back my chair with a metallic squeal and the dog swivels his head to look at me. He does not fret so much now when he is inside, on a soft place. He will sleep an hour or so, as long as I am close by, but always wakes with a grand expectation.

Well, are we gonna do sumthin'. Let's DO sumthin'.

I still hate to read too much into a dog, but I'll bet you a hundred dollars that's it.

"Come on," I say. "Let's go see the codger."

He knows this means food, because he has never been in her presence longer than two minutes without eating. He looks at the door the way I look at the buffet at a Western Sizzlin.

"You are the sorriest dog in the whole, wide world," I tell him as we clomp up the stairs, where he gets his first postbreakfast snack of the day.

And it occurs to me, watching the old woman drop treats into his teeth, that I have made it through a whole morning without even thinking of this never-ending dread called COVID-19.

"Come on, let's go outside," I say, but he doesn't budge until the old woman closes the refrigerator door, then reaches down to pet his head, and tells him what a good boy he is.

"He really is good," she says.

"Who you tryin' to convince?" I ask her.

We bang through the screen door and out into the yard, where it occurs to me, like it does every day, that there is really nowhere to go. Even the Huddle House is closed, and walking through a crowd can get you killed. We watched it happen in the big cities, and now we wait for it to find us here. The long, winding driveway has been, in a way, never more beautiful. But even as we found a kind of safety out here, I knew that the old woman had paid a high price for it. Held prisoner here, exiled into the middle of all this space and all this worry, the old woman found herself very much alone.

•

In the span of about six months, the last of her siblings, the last of her Great Family, passed away. Her sister Jo, who talked to her every night before she went to bed, passed away, followed just months later by my uncle John, and then her sister Juanita, her best friend for eighty years. They were the last links to her mother and father and sisters and brothers who had passed on. They were all buried quickly, quietly, without the attention, the traditions, they deserved, the way people always are in a time of plague.

"I'm all that's left, ain't I?" said my mother, and I think it was the loneliest thing I ever heard.

I was not the one who needed a dog right now. I had rented him to my brother when he needed him, though he never actually came across with any *cash*. Now I loaned him to my mother, for free. It was not really a job for a young dog, one that could never sit around and listen to an old woman talk about the dead, but then he wasn't such a young dog anymore.

•

He was seven or eight by then, maybe a little older, though I guess we will never know for sure. He still did pretty much every irritating thing he did when he first got here almost three years ago, but at three-quarter speed. The cats sometimes didn't even bother to climb a tree anymore, just ran away till he got tired and stopped, and looked at him, hissing, spitting, baleful. *Stupid dog.* He could still take the jackasses for a spin, though now it was mostly just a lope. He still tried to terrorize UPS, FedEx, and the metermen, but they were all onto him by now, and when he came roaring into the yard to confront them, they just gave him a treat and walked on by.

He was good company, now, for her.

I tried to talk to my mom, in that awful time. But she didn't need someone to talk with, I soon learned. She just needed a listener. And as the summer of 2020 burned away, the dog lay on the couch or at her knee and listened, between naps, between snacks, as the old woman talked. He stayed with her not minutes but hours, though I admit that depended on what he heard outside on his mountain. It was probably just the heat, just an escape from it, for a dog getting older, a dog slowing down. But it was kind of nice, as sad as it was, to stand in that doorway, and watch.

She talked for hours, whether I was in the room or not. It *was* a Great Family, one that lived in fifteen houses in fourteen years, fleeing landlords, rolling through the mountains like gypsies, a kind of tin-pot royalty, as she recalled. She talked about her daddy, who worked on the rooftops with a hammer in his hand and in the mountains stoking up a copper still, and about her mother, who had hair dark as ten feet down, and loved that man. She talked about her brothers, of James, who could out-lie any man in Calhoun County, and William, who once tied her up in an onion sack and hung it from a tree. She talked of Sue, who was still beautiful when she got the cancer, and

Edna, who sewed uniforms at Fort McClellan and was the second-best cook in the world. But mostly she talked of Jo, who married John the year I was born, and Juanita, her best friend, who drove us to the Gulf in a yellow '63 Biscayne, and busted Sue's windshield with a hammer, because she was by God mad.

She had photographs, of course, but she couldn't see them. But she could still see inside her own mind. So the old woman, the dog, and I sheltered at the end of the long driveway, and yet flew all over the highlands, from one shack to another, across cotton fields and fish camps, trading in one old jalopy for another, always moving.

I was not worried about her mind. She will be making sense when the rest of us are wearing little paper birthday hats in the home, and when she talked to the dog, alone, it made perfect sense to me. Sometimes he even followed her into the kitchen and sprawled on the floor as she cooked, breaking her strictest taboo, of having such a nasty creature in her kitchen. She just stepped over him, still talking, till one day she was just done, the story complete in her own heart. And when she went to sleep at night, the dog climbed onto the foot of her bed, as if he was waiting for the rest of the story.

•

I came home one day to find the bad dog piled up on the couch watching *Gunsmoke* with her. This time, I thought, I might not get him back.

"He likes the cows," she said, motioning to the screen, where a bellowing mob of Herefords was thundering unchecked down the main street of Dodge.

"He might not like the gunfire," I said, since someone got shot every twenty-three minutes, usually Marshal Matt Dillon himself. He had been shot 744 times, 363 in the same shoulder.

She made a dismissive wave of her hand.

"He knows the difference between real shootin' and TV shootin'; watch and see if he don't," she said, and I watched as the dog didn't even twitch or cover his eyes when Marshal Dillon sent someone to Boot Hill with two shots from a .44.

"See."

I came in another afternoon and he was sitting in my brother's favorite leather chair, listening to a televangelist.

He was uninterested in the preaching; it was loud and accusing and strident, and messed with his afternoon nap in the cool of the air-conditioning, but he perked up, she said, when the choir walked out.

"He just likes the singing," she said.

"Me, too," I said, and we sat there till it was done, till my mother leaned close to the TV and placed her hands on the screen, asking the man inside the glass to pray for my brother Sam. The dog just watched her, a good boy, for at least a while, and then he got a little bored during the love offering and went and scratched at the door.

•

Don't misunderstand me. He was still a terrible dog. But his sense of sadness and struggle was so sharp I sometimes just watched him, amazed, and I had to share him with the people who needed him most. I didn't need a dog as badly as they did.

But all I had to do was sit down on the steps, at the end of that long driveway, and he was my dog again. He thumped up the steps and used his nose to lift my arm up to where it rested on his shoulders, and I was all right, and I guess he was, too.

SIXTEEN

Boomers

THUNDER is different here. It does not roll along the landscape like most places, marching closer and closer across the flatland. Here the low mountains hide the horizon and mute the sound, so sometimes you think you *might* hear a storm, *believe* you do, somewhere off toward Ohatchee, but you can't be sure. But the dog is. Sometimes I think the dog can hear that distant boom coming, even with his mismatched, glued-on ears, as far as the Talladega County line.

He dashes up on the porch and stares at the doorknob till someone notices him there and lets him in the house. My mother opens the door to the basement and he comes quietly, slowly down the steps, almost crawling, and slinks over to sit by my desk, to nudge my leg and lick my hand.

The cabin, cut from twelve-inch cedar beams and half buried in the mountain itself, is about as safe a place as there is, and still we can hear it shake. The thunder comes rushing, crashing through the holler like a train hurtling through a tunnel; I used to laugh at that old cliché, but there's just nothing else that comes close to that sound. The normally fearless dog panics and runs around the place, ducking into the bedroom closet, in and out of the bathtub, but always settling on the foot of the bed. He builds himself a place to hide, pawing together quilts and pillows into a kind of cave, and though I know I should chase him off it I don't have the heart. He pokes his face out, shaking, and it always makes me think of that weak, hurt, starved, unwanted dog.

In that goofy language that develops between a boy and his dog, we have named them "boomers." A boomer can't hurt him, I tell him, and I get up and sit on the foot of the bed and rub his head. I don't know if he understands what I am saying, but I know for damn sure he doesn't believe me. And he looks at me like I could fix it, if I wanted to.

Good boy, I tell him, and that is the best I can do.

And it always breaks my heart a little, to see him reduced to just that, to just a good boy.

•

This fall will mark his third anniversary here. I think we will call it a birthday, since he started over here, in a way. It seems a lot longer than that.

We mark time by visits to the vet. We have to go every three months, for maintenance and repairs. I would learn there is a lot more of that, on a dog like mine. I took him in once when he seemed sluggish, but it turned out he was just feeling *blah,* and wanted an egg biscuit. Then I drove him past some cows, out at the dairy in Alexandria on Highway 431, and he was all right again. A few weeks ago, he got into a mysterious fight on the mountain and something split the bottom of his right ear, a wound too long and deep for a housecat. He got a shot, antibiotics, and a corn dog.

Sam said he had seen bobcats mark up a dog that way. So maybe he found one more bobcat out there after all.

"He wouldn't know to leave it alone," he said, "would he?"

"No," I said. "He wouldn't know."

The terrible cough from his damaged trachea has reoccurred, but only once in a while and usually for only a moment. I looked into a surgery to repair it, but the procedure could be dangerous, and didn't always work. The vet said it was best to treat it as it reoccurred, and let him live his life. But if it came back and did not ease, if it threatened his life, I'd pay anything to save him.

Till then, I held to what he told me that first time.

Dogs have an amazing ability to start over, to reset.

I wonder how many dogs, in the short arc of their lives, have reset the way this one has? How many dogs, with such a tenuous grip on their own life, have touched the people around them as he has? I know I said, over and over, there was no magic in it, and I am not a man who goes through this life looking for evidence of fate, or karma, or listening for the flutter of angels.

He is just something that happened to us, in a time of loss and sadness and sickness and uncertainty, when, as the boy Little Arliss said in *Old Yeller,* we needed us a dog.

"I don't know, Momma, maybe he's just bad luck," I told her, not long ago. I remember the dog had buttermilk and crumbled cornbread on his face, and she went to get a paper towel, to clean him up. I was looking at it wrong, she said, as she wiped his face like he was a four-year-old. Think, she said, if the mean old world just kept turning, turning, and we didn't have him at all.

•

He is a terrible burden, or at least that is something I have come to say. I guess the truth is that he does not truly ask for much in return. He just wants some people of his own, and some snacks, because a dog gets used to things like that. He wants a big, tangled place to run and hunt, and if it happens to be overrun with jackasses he will do his best to keep them in check, though you know how they can be. He wants a place to lie, a place outside where he can hear and smell the mountain as he closes his eyes, and wants a booger to battle deep in the black trees. And he wants someone to come let him in, when the thunder shakes the mountain, when the lightning flash reveals that he was just a dog all this time, just a dog after all.

Light Sleeper

M E, I'm doing all right.
Compared to what everyone else has been dealt, on this mountain, I've got it made.

I have work to do, and people to look after even as they look after me. And as long as I am not left alone with my thoughts for too long, I have found that—much of the time—this river of melancholy is really just a noise, a rushing sound, like that ringing in my ears.

I have made one last promise, to help look after my mom and my brothers and the ones they love. It is no more or less than most people manage. I ain't expecting accolades.

I would have liked to stick my toes in the sand, or ride a tall horse. Today, I will go buy fifty pounds of cat food, and like it.

We got my brother a new tractor last week, one that will not scald him, one that rides like a Cadillac. The dog peed on it, first thing, but I do not believe anyone was looking.

I lean on a fence post sometimes and just watch my big brother trundle across the wide pasture. He does not seem to be going anyplace in particular, and he does not have to be, I suppose. Some men just prefer the view from the seat of a tractor. I always thought that was kind of wonderful, to know, absolutely, what made you happy.

"Sometimes I just like to hear something run," he said. "That's all it takes."

I lean on that fence post and listen till I hear him make the turn at the barbed wire and head back, and I know that everything is all right for another day. I turn and head back up the hill and am surprised, even after all this time, to feel the dog bump against my leg, walking almost in step.

"Let's go to the house," I say.

He bounces, not as high as he used to.

We run up the hill, me so slow he loops around me three, four times, like I don't have sense enough to find my way to the cabin by myself. And to think, I used to think *he* was stupid.

•

One more seemingly endless summer has finally died, thrashing. It was a hard summer on the old folks. My people used to say that, all the time . . . *hard on the old folks* . . .

"The fall will be better," I say to the dog, and before it is out of my mouth I almost choke on it. I don't say silly, optimistic stuff like that, but maybe the dog is wearing off on me.

I look down to see if he is listening, but I am just talking to the wind. It happens more and more these days, as he skulks away and leaves me yammering in the trees.

He is pawing in the vines near the pond, and I limp down to find him scratching at a small, dead snake, a copperhead, I think. It is hard to tell. The head is missing. They will be out, down here, till the leaves turn. Leave it to Speck to find the last snake of the year.

I panic, again, and drag him up the hill. I am pretty sure it will be my last act on earth, dragging a stupid dog up a stupid hill. I take him into the house and, under a strong light, roll him over and over, looking for a bite. Nothing.

He thinks I am playing, and rolls over onto his back, for a belly rub.

"Quit that," my mother says. She still, after all this time, considers it indecent.

He lolls, wild-eyed.

"Show some manners," she says.

His tongue dangles out the side of his mouth.

Then, his job here complete, he bolts for the scarred kitchen door. He will have to be there to greet the tractor, which he still does not trust. It is bright orange, too close to red to suit him, so he herds it into the yard and then into its stall, till the rumbling stops. I think he believes it has gone to sleep.

●

The fall will be easier. The holidays, beginning with the first glowing orange pumpkins, have always lifted my heart, though I know this year will be different. The season of corona lingers, with no real hope in sight. But it is the South, where a goodly number of people consider it a hoax anyway, and people seem determined to ignore it with a belligerence unique to my people; as for me and mine, not being ignorant, we wear masks, and my mother surrounds us with a bubble of prayer, which I appreciate even as my pants begin to smolder. It seems odd to just go on living, celebrating, but also seems wrong to let it cheat us out of the seasons we have left.

Around the cabin, you can smell woodsmoke on the breeze. The people burn their brush piles a day or two after the first chilly rain, build their first fires in the fireplace. As much as the red and gold leaves on the mountainside, it is how you know the holidays are coming near. Sometimes, when the wind is just right, you can hear the marching bands in town on Friday and Saturday nights, see the faint glow of stadium lights. They would still play football here if bubonic plague infected the land, if old men rang bells and walked the streets while chanting "Bring out your dead." But people here are sick of it all, just want things to be better, and some never believed much in science, anyway. We grow them that way, here. Bless their hearts.

The scientists warn it could get worse, much worse, this late fall and winter, and I look around me at the faces in town or in the doctor's office and I see a look I recognize too well; it's my look, that look of tired melancholy. Everyone keeps walking, waiting, beside that damn river. I want to yell out, tell them to go find a bad dog, but I know that's not the cure they are looking for.

But it couldn't hurt.

In a time when the days seem twice as long and the whole world drags, could it hurt to go out and find every awful, hopeless dog on every dirty street and desolate country road, and give them a home? I mean, what if you had a few million rescued dogs, ripping up the days?

•

My mother tells me to begin watching the grocery stores for good deals on a frozen turkey; it will need to be a big one, since we have to allow for Speck. He ate so much last Thanksgiving he went into a brief coma.

I scratch out a Christmas list with an old reporter's notebook and a No. 2 pencil. It is shorter this year; the Great Family is smaller. All the more reason not to waste it.

My people like old-fashioned things, like gold crosses and good pocketknives, thick sweatshirts and good socks. They like food they would not buy for themselves, like tins of dates, figs, Brazil nuts, pecans, walnuts, cashews, and Georgia peanuts, and boxes of fudge, chocolate-covered cherries, and fruitcakes, the fancy kind soaked in whiskey. It is the only liquor that has ever passed my mother's lips.

I show my mother the list and she reads and nods till she gets to the end.

"What about the dog?"

"I figured you could just stomp him another jug," I say.

She sends me back to my room with my pencil, like a child.

Speck's List, I scrawl.

Sliced ham
Sliced turkey
Sliced chicken
Cocktail weenies
Seven rubber balls (six to bury, one to chew)
New collar with fluorescent stripe
Greenies
Assorted treats
Giant bone stuffed with peanut butter
Dog bed

I scratched that last one out, then wrote it back in. It has been years since he ate the last one. Maybe he has changed. Then I went back and scratched it out again.

●

I still suffer from all the ailments of Job. I still feel, some days, like I have been visited by everything but locusts, that there is no joy in this sorry ol' life . . . but in the midst of such stark, real suffering I shut my mouth. The only one who really knows my mind is raising hell out in the weeds and trees. We talk every night on the steps outside the kitchen door, and when I cannot sleep we talk again, sometimes into the early morning, or till he hears a booger out there in the dark and crashes up the mountain after it. I won't go inside while he is out there, and sometimes I nod off there on the steps and only wake up when he sticks his cold nose in my ear or in my eye. I look him over in the yellow glow of the porch light, to make sure that, this time, it was not a bear, and then I stagger up the steps to go to bed, banging against at least one of the door jams. I hold the door open, in case he should want to sleep on the couch, but he just trots off to his place by the gate, to wait on the next rustling of the leaves or creaking of the pines. The bad dog is a light sleeper; I can just raise my hand, sometimes, and the rustle of cloth will wake him.

"Goodnight, buddy," I always say, then, always, "I'll see you in the morning."

I say it like I have some control over it all. Most nights, before I close my eyes, I hear a ruckus out there in the leaves, hear that urgent bark, and I stumble out the door, to rescue some innocent possum, or treed cat, or just to poke my head out

the door so he will see me and know that I have
registered his diligence, that I have entered it
into whatever ledger it is he thinks I keep; he just
knows for sure there is one.

Did you see me?

And he knows he will never be invisible, again.

•

The bad dog rang in the new year by destroying
the ligaments in his left, rear leg. I do not know
how. He may have been fighting something, again,
out there in the wild and dark, or just wrenched it
violently trying to free himself from some snag. Or
maybe, the vet said, it was hereditary, one more
defect in my defective dog.

So, they put him back together, again.

"This was accomplished," read the vet's synopsis
of the procedure, "by grafting a portion of the
patella tendon in place of the anterior cruciate
ligament, transposing the biceps femoris insertion,
and implanting a nylon stay suture to support the
knee while the graft is healing . . . It is imperative
that your pet's activity be severely limited during
the healing process."

I looked at the dog. He looked at me.

"I think this means you're a goner," I told him.

237

He was good for a few days, or maybe he was just hurting. My mother let him sleep at the foot of her bed, and covered him with a tiny heirloom quilt she had used to cover her only grandchild, my niece, Meredith, when she was a baby.

He tore it into scraps and string.

That night, he escaped out the front door, and went hopping, limping, and yowling into the dark. I ran him down, and when he fought at the leash I toted him, squirming, glaring, into the house.

For weeks now, he has watched the door, and waited for his chance to escape. Sometimes he makes it and sometimes he doesn't. But I catch him. I am faster than him, now; I am a leaf on the wind.

"After twelve weeks, your pet can resume normal activity," the vet wrote.

Normal.

Yeah.

We'll wait for that.

No cats were harmed in the making of this book.

Acknowledgments

There would have been no story without these people, for there would have been no dog. I would like to thank

Pam,
Mary,
Angie,
Danielle,
Dr. Ryan, and
Dr. Clanton

They kept my terrible dog alive.